THE

≡Ⅱ ERNST &

ENTREPRENEUR
OF THE YEAR®
AWARD
INSIGHTS FROM THE
WINNER'S CIRCLE

GREGORY K. ERICKSEN

D **rborn**™
Trade Publishing
A **Kaplan Professional** Company

This publication is designed to provide accurate and authoritative information in regard to the subject matter covered. It is sold with the understanding that the publisher is not engaged in rendering legal, accounting, or other professional service. If legal advice or other expert assistance is required, the services of a competent professional person should be sought.

Vice President and Publisher: Cynthia A. Zigmund
Editorial Director: Donald J. Hull
Acquisitions Editor: Mary B. Good
Senior Managing Editor: Jack Kiburz
Interior Design: Lucy Jenkins
Cover Design: Scott Rattray, Rattray Design
Typesetting: Elizabeth Pitts

Entrepreneur of the Year® is a registered trademark of Ernst & Young LLP.

Published by Dearborn Trade Publishing, a Kaplan Professional Company

Printed in the United States of America

02 03 04 10 9 8 7 6 5 4 3 2 1

Library of Congress Cataloging-in-Publication Data

Ericksen, Gregory K.
   The Ernst & Young Entrepreneur of the Year Award insights from the winner's circle / Gregory K. Ericksen.
      p.   cm.
Includes index.
   ISBN 0-7931-4889-8
1. Entrepreneurship.   2. New business enterprises—Management.
I. Title: Ernst and Young Entrepreneur of the Year Award insights from the winner's circle.   II. Title.
   HB615 .E745 2002
   658.4'21—dc21

                                                                    2001006509

CONTENTS

MEET THE JUDGES: The Ernst & Young Entrepreneur Of The Year® Featured Judges

Olympians win Gold Medals. Actors and actresses are honored at Cannes or the Academy Awards. Scientists vie for the Nobel Prize. But for business achievement, the pinnacle is Ernst & Young's Entrepreneur Of The Year® Award.

Real business champions must master an intricate combination of many different skills and strengths, and—when they are tested in the fire of entrepreneurship—they must perform these skills consistently and superbly over long stretches of time. The Entrepreneur Of The Year (EOY) judges, many of whom are previous honorees, know a champion when they see one and know how to help you become a champion, too.

In this book, EOY judges explain how they started and managed successful companies, what criteria they use to evaluate the Entrepreneur Of The Year contenders, what practices the most effective entrepreneurs follow, and how your business can meet these criteria by using similar concepts.

These judges are standard bearers because of their accomplishments as entrepreneurs, as the creators and chief executives of high growth businesses that make significant contributions to their communities. They have already survived the scrutiny of EOY competition and triumphed.

Here, Entrepreneur Of The Year judges reveal exactly what they look for when assessing companies and entrepreneurs. This will give you the knowledge you need to examine your own endeavor with their clear-eyed sense of purpose. You are invited to put your business under the same microscope. But this is not only a diagnostic exam—it is the gateway to action, to moving your company forward.

This book begins with its title chapter, "You Be the Judge: Inside the Process," a firsthand tour of the deliberative, thorough judging process. Judges explain the key criteria they use—the six categories in which every Entrepreneur Of The Year winner must excel. You have a front-row seat inside the competition, so you can participate from the perspective of both the entrepreneurs and the judges. The cultural context of this competition, a 17-year-old adventure in entrepreneurship, is the context of business itself: brilliant ideas, rapid change, uncertain times, great opportunities and hard practicalities.

The judges reveal their criteria, step-by-step, and offer relevant advice, illustrated by corporate case histories, in four chapters covering leadership, team building, innovation, and finance.

In "Leadership: Make It So," the judges explain how to put your entrepreneurial spirit to work toward concrete accomplishment. This challenging task requires vision, passion, commitment, and risk taking, all focused strategically. In the words of Star Trek Captain Jean Luc Picard, leadership is the ability to take your dream and "make it so."

In "Team Building: Putting People First," the judges set out the managerial practices that lead to the alignment, profitability, and longevity they expect from EOY companies. They emphasize building a strong management team, including advisors, boards of directors, and executives. Next, the judges discuss serving the rest of your company's stakeholders: your employees, your customers, and your community. They describe successful methods EOY winners use to attract, reward, and retain productive, effective workers. In this evaluation, they show you how developing a cohesive corporate culture and providing meaningful community service benefits your company and your bottom line.

"Innovation: Breaking the Mold" discusses how entrepreneurs must embody creativity and implement originality throughout their organizations. Judges talk about innovation as it applies at the beginning of a venture and during the company's continued survival and growth. Innovation also demands the ability to inspire, to adapt, to diversify, to change to be flexible, and to overcome adversity—so the judges explain how to put those difficult skills to work.

In the final chapter, "Financial Performance: Money Matters," EOY judges reward entrepreneurs who create long-lasting growth and profitable businesses based on wise planning and strategic thinking. The judges aren't shy about praising strong financial practices and condemning weak ones, such as stubborn refusal to adjust to changing circumstances.

The Entrepreneur Of The Year judges note that selection criteria categories are always fluid. Excellent entrepreneurship crosses the lines between categories. Traits that help an entrepreneur craft a winning fiscal strategy might also boost his or her ability to set up an innovative supply line or establish an effective employee incentive program.

But, in the end, it doesn't matter that the key categories blend or overlap. According to the judges, entrepreneurs win EOY recognition only if they perform superbly in every arena.

Many books, Web sites, and academic studies cover the management secrets of entrepreneurs, but the EOY judges add a distinguished and distinctive voice to this discourse. Not only are they award-winning businesspeople, but they have also studied other successful business leaders. They are graduates of the hands-on "University of Entrepreneurship," with a deep understanding of how entrepreneurs start with ideas and create enduring businesses.

Each year, EOY judges sort through the detailed applications of thousands of worthy candidates to identify each year's leading regional entrepreneurs and the Entrepreneur Of The Year. After learning how the judges assess performance and what winning entrepreneurs actually do, you can go back to your desk, examine your business, and understand, starting now, that you too can be a champion.

Gregory K. Ericksen
Ernst & Young
Global Director
Entrepreneur Of The Year

ACKNOWLEDGMENTS

I am most grateful to the many judges over the years who have generously given their energy, wisdom, and insight to Ernst & Young's Entrepreneur Of The Year program. Their contributions to the program—and their support of entrepreneurship around the globe—are inestimable. For editorial support, thanks go to Michelle Puleio, Ed Wakin, Andrea Mackiewicz, and Nancy Clark. I also appreciate Ernst & Young Chairman Jim Turley's ongoing support in recognition of that special breed of people known the world over as entrepreneurs. Thank you all.

CHAPTER 1

You Be the Judge

INSIDE THE PROCESS

"I'm a practicing CEO who runs a holding company that has 22

different businesses, yet when I come as a judge and study some of

the best companies in the world, I can't help but be a student. I

constantly learn things that I can take back to make our practices

even better. So I approach the judging from the standpoint of a

student of business, still learning as much as I can possibly learn.

Through the judging process, where I get to see so many companies, I

get to review the cream of the crop."

—JUDGE JACK STACK

The Ernst & Young Entrepreneur Of The Year judges use six key criteria to gauge a corporate leader's performance. Because these six factors shape the competition, the judging, and the work of the entrepreneurs, they are presented here first. So examine these pivotal criteria, and then step inside the workings of the competition itself to meet the judges and your colleagues, some very competitive, very intriguing entrepreneurs.

But first a few words about why this competition exists and why this information matters to you: As the business environment becomes increasingly challenging, we look to people who have proven their ability to go up against the odds as they created and directed successful companies. We look to entrepreneurs for the knowledge they demonstrate in seeing optimistic opportunity where others see turmoil and chaos.

We can learn valuable lessons from entrepreneurs about ingenuity, resourcefulness, perseverance, and overcoming adversity. Entrepreneurs start something new, encounter unpredictable circumstances, and still find the motivation and strength to move forward. They can show us how to manage in periods of uncertainty.

Throughout this text, the war stories of entrepreneurs' actual achievements are used to illustrate the possibilities that become open to you when you start a new venture or run a business.

The entrepreneurs you will hear from and read about in this book are in a class by themselves. They are distinguished winners of the Ernst & Young Entrepreneur Of The Year Award, the most prestigious honor that individuals can earn for starting and managing successful businesses. Remarkably, almost every Entrepreneur Of The Year (EOY) story in this book involves a business that took root during the tumultuous height of the Information Age and triumphed during the birth pangs of the Connected Economy. As a result, EOY winners exemplify superb achievement during an era of revolution and uncertainty.

When you meet EOY winners who have graduated into the roles of award judges, you are meeting the senior professors of entrepreneurship. The Entrepreneur Of The Year judges provide a unique and valuable perspective. As the admired founder-leaders of outstanding companies, they have "walked the talk." They used their own experiences, built their own networks, and trusted their own instincts to forge brilliant entrepreneurial careers and build internationally important enterprises.

In this book, the judges "talk the walk" for you. They introduce the six keys they use to evaluate the success of entrepreneurs and their businesses during the Entrepreneur Of The Year judging roundtables. And they generously reveal their own corporate and personal journeys as they teach you the principles and insights they bring to bear as judges.

THE SIX KEYS TO SUCCESS

If you are action oriented, you can plan and manage your business using EOY's Six Keys to Winning, which were developed almost a decade after the program began in 1986. The keys were created by compiling many judges' input on the characteristics and indicators they seek when they are assessing an entrepreneur. We then interviewed many Entrepreneur Of The Year judges and eventually detected a pattern in their criteria. After testing this hypothesis through two rounds of national judging, we grouped the judges' evaluations into six categories. The six keys are now the standard way that EOY judges group their observations and discussions about an entrepreneur's merits.

1. Leadership

Do the entrepreneurs have a vision to which they are committed; are they passionate about what they do; are they calculated risk-takers; and do they grow personally as their companies grow? Are they strategic about their actions? Do the entrepreneurs set high standards for themselves and their companies? Do they demonstrate an unflinching desire and determination to succeed? Do they rely on trusted individuals but still retain the capacity to think independently and to take risks in the face of uncertainty? Do the entrepreneurs turn business visions into business realities? These criteria are covered in the chapter on leadership.

2. Financial Performance

Have the entrepreneurs built enterprises that make money and grow, as evidenced by solid metrics such as revenue and profitability? Does financial performance indicate that their companies use professional planning and manage for the long term? What is their track record for raising financing, making quality investments, and providing for long-term sustainability? These criteria are covered in the chapter on financial performance.

3. Management Team

As their companies grow, have these entrepreneurs ensured continued success by assembling a management team of high-quality people, including executives, advisors, and boards of directors? Do they demonstrate entrepreneurial maturity by building strategic alliances and surrounding themselves with talented people? Do they build and rebuild their teams' commitment to common goals? These criteria are covered in the chapter on team building.

4. Culture, Values, and Incentives

Have the entrepreneurs created workplace environments in which employees are respected, recognized, and rewarded for their individual and team contributions? Have they created a corporate culture that is customer focused and that encourages giving back to their communities? Do the entrepreneurs live their values? Do they have the ability to communicate ideas and the potential to influence others? These criteria also are covered in the chapter on team building.

5. Originality

Do the entrepreneurs consistently use creativity and innovation to help their businesses thrive? Are they flexible, diversified, and adaptable? Do they recognize the business imperative of anticipating and embracing change within a culture of innovation? Are their business practices and products original? Have they pioneered a new approach or technology? Do they pay attention to continuous improvement and innovation in all aspects of their businesses? These criteria are covered in the chapter on innovation.

6. Degree of Difficulty

Did the entrepreneurs overcome obstacles or adversity as they launched and built their businesses? Have they confronted personal adversity and triumphed as creative individuals? Do they demonstrate perseverance in the face of trouble? These criteria also are covered in the chapter on innovation.

The six keys are designed to be universal. They apply across industries and are appropriate measurements for companies at every stage of growth. For example, financial performance matters whether you run a restaurant or manufacture turbine engines: you can't stay in business unless you make a profit. The six keys are also flexible, because the factors that denote success can change over time and are different in differ-ent industries, countries, and circumstances.

The judges' criteria go beyond the six keys. For example, at the level of the World Entrepreneur Of The Year competition, these criteria still matter greatly but other criteria also come into play. Along with the criteria on finance and innovation, the judges' ballot for World Entrepreneur Of The Year adds evalu-ations of entrepreneurial spirit, strategic direction, and per-sonal integrity and influence, which are intrinsic to the judging on all levels. World competitors must also show global impact, which means creating an organization that is truly interna-tional, with worldwide investors, clients, and concerns.

EOY judges ask these contenders how they have expanded their operations and markets to include international activi-ties. Are they making a global impact in terms of job creation and improved living economics? Or do they have solid plans to expand internationally? Are they aware of globalization issues, and are they adopting forward-looking, effective policies?

All six major EOY criteria create a lively competition. When entrepreneurs go head-to-head for Entrepreneur Of The Year, whether regionally, nationally, or globally, everyone in-volved is challenged. The competition has to be fair, organized, and logical. The judges have to be clearheaded, hardworking, well informed, and diligent. And the entrepreneurs have to be at the peak of their performance.

First, step inside the competition.

THE ENTREPRENEUR OF THE YEAR AWARDS PROGRAM

Ernst & Young started the Entrepreneur Of The Year pro-gram on a small scale in 1986, with EOY Award ceremonies in a few regions of the United States. By 2002, the program was active in over 100 cities worldwide and in over 30 countries on six continents.

Just during the short life span of this program, business has undergone a tremendous upheaval spurred by technology and shifts in global culture. Information age technology has been adopted with amazing rapidity, sparking a business revolution. The contemplative time that resulted from communication by letter was shortened first by the fax and then by computers, cell phones, and e-mail. Today, the Global Positioning Satellite system makes it possible to get a business call while you're climbing Mount Everest. In the new century's intense environment, business never stops.

As Intel's chairman Andy Grove explains: "Leaders have to act . . . more quickly today. The pressure to act that comes from employees, shareholders, and directors comes much faster than it did five to ten years ago because information is available in a much shorter time."

The enterprising, flexible, innovative entrepreneur is critically important in a business culture that moves so quickly. That may help to explain the global welcome that the Entrepreneur Of The Year program received steadily as it expanded over the past 17 years.

Government and business leaders around the world recognize and support the positive impact that entrepreneurs have on local communities and national economies. In recognition of the importance of entrepreneurs, such organizations as CNN, the Nasdaq stock market, *USA Today,* and the Ewing Marion Kauffman Foundation's Center for Entrepreneurial Leadership work with Ernst & Young as supporters of the Entrepreneur Of The Year Awards.

Because this program is a global benchmark of entrepreneurship, leaders around the world use it to embrace the culture of entrepreneurship. They see the Entrepreneur Of The Year Award as a way to honor indigenous business leaders and create national role models. Now that national winners compete to be named World Entrepreneur Of The Year, the global business community has the means to unite in support of the concept of principled entrepreneurial excellence.

Each Entrepreneur Of The Year Award cycle lasts for a year. In the United States, for example, the nomination process begins in December and January. Anyone who is associated with a successful entrepreneur can nominate a candidate; this includes spouses, employees, bankers, public relations managers, or entrepreneurs themselves. In fact, the competition encourages self-nominations. After all, no one knows the dimensions of an entrepreneur's success better than the entrepreneur. All nominations, which are confidential, are submitted to the independent panels of judges. In 2001 more than 8,000 entrepreneurs were nominated worldwide.

A nominee must be an owner/manager primarily responsible for the recent performance of a company that is at least two years old. Founders of public companies are eligible if they are still active in top management. Anyone who has made an outstanding contribution to the entrepreneurial spirit or has helped an entrepreneur succeed—whether through business, economic, or academic means—is eligible for the National Supporter of Entrepreneurship Award presented by the Kauffman Center for Entrepreneurial Leadership.

Complete nominations for Entrepreneur Of The Year are due in April so that regional judging sessions can be held in May; regional award banquets are in June. All regional winners are inducted into the Entrepreneur Of The Year Hall of Fame, part of the Entrepreneur Of The Year Academy, which was created to celebrate entrepreneurial accomplishments and to make the general public more aware of entrepreneurs' contributions. National judging sessions for the upcoming year's national winners are held in August, with the Award Gala held each year during the annual Entrepreneur Of The Year Awards in Palm Springs, California.

The World Entrepreneur Of The Year Award Gala, which is hosted for the previous year's national winners from countries around the world, is held every June in Monte Carlo. At the 2002 gathering, 22 national winners were eligible for the award, which was won by Stefan Vilsmeier, the German neurological software entrepreneur who founded BrainLAB GmbH.

U.S. Entrepreneur Of The Year nominees can anticipate a whirlwind year of activity and celebration even as they continue to manage their companies successfully. Regional awards precede national gatherings, culminating in Palm Springs, where each regional winner undergoes the rigors of the Ernst & Young on-site interview for national recognition. The judges consider individual and company dossiers, analyze candidates based on the six key criteria, and debate the merits of the entrepreneurs with their fellow judges.

Even if the debate can get "mildly heated," as one judge described it, the judges are united in their determination to reach a fair conclusion. They have a purpose beyond picking a winner: in choosing the Entrepreneur Of The Year, the judges also define what makes a great entrepreneur. Judging also means accepting responsibility for maintaining the integrity of the EOY Award Program.

Inacomp Corporation founder and CEO Rick Inatome, who is a former EOY winner and a judge, explains: "How we define an entrepreneur is what we do as national judges of this program. We should interpret the word *entrepreneur* to keep it in line with the evolving scenario of the American economy. We are a reflection point for the country."

Steve Papermaster, chairman of Powershift Group and a 1996 regional Entrepreneur Of The Year, says this is a very individualized process. "You can't create a cookie cutter for the successful entrepreneur," he explains.

The Entrepreneur Of The Year Award is a barometer of excellence, particularly when the economic atmosphere is in flux. For example, during the dot-com boom, judges were challenged to reconsider the weight they gave to their evaluations of the financial performance of e-businesses.

After all, the argument went, hadn't venture capitalists, financial analysts, and other experts already loosened or shifted their valuations and their expectations? By the end of the debate, the judges decided to be guided by a common value they have propagated since the EOY program began. They decided that every winner must demonstrate that he or she has made a profit and built a company that is designed to last.

They determined that the EOY Award should not go to flash-in-the-pan companies or to people who were trying to get rich quick. As a result, all of the U.S. national winners during the dot-com years were entrepreneurs whose ventures had been around at least two years, as requested by the application criteria. In addition, the winners' companies were profitable, a criteria every Entrepreneur Of The Year must meet.

"Being a judge is a tremendous education and certainly a privilege.

I can't help but turn the judgment on myself and ask, 'How do I really

rate in this group of contemporaries?'"

—JUDGE REBECCA SMITH

JUDGMENT DAY

Nominations are sorted according to the nominee's industry—construction and real estate, health sciences, manufacturing, retailing, services, and technology and communications—and they are judged in industry groups in each region. Winners proceed to a national competition in countries where regional competitions are held.

At the national level, a panel of one facilitator and three judges—generally former winners in the industry being judged—begins with a stack of nominations and tries to whittle them down to three finalists for group discussion, although paring down these groups of accomplished individuals is a tough job. Judges who are not EOY winners are experts who come from academia, business, and the media.

A few years ago, the selection of all national winners was scheduled to take place on a single day, although that timing varies. In this particular case, the industry panels met in the morning. Meanwhile, two additional sets of judges convened to select winners in the special Master Entrepreneur and Supporter of Entrepreneurship categories, which were tantamount to lifetime achievement awards. Some years, awards are granted for such cross-industry categories, depending on the pool of candidates. Occasionally, awards are granted in various other categories, including Young Entrepreneur, Emerging Entrepreneur, and e-Business Entrepreneur.

Each independent regional and national judging panel has the sole discretion to select the categories and award recipients based on the quality and quantity of the nominations received.

MEET THE JUDGES

*W*hen you are the entrepreneur or the leader of a company, your responsibility is to do the right thing, be a good person, and be a leader, whether you are trekking around the grocery store, working in the yard, or at a White House State Dinner. You are always representing an image that is what people will associate with your company.

—**REBECCA SMITH**, Founder and President of the A.D. Morgan Corporation

Rebecca Smith founded and grew A.D. Morgan Corporation during a time when failed construction companies were the rule rather than the exception. Her firm maintains an outstanding reputation in the construction industry for construction managers and general contractors.

Smith attributes her success to "projects finished on time, within budget, and without confusion and complexities created in the field. It is nothing more than old-fashioned service delivered by a very talented and energetic team that is supported by the latest computerized equipment and management systems."

The A.D. Morgan project experience is diverse, including educational projects, corrections and detention facilities, health care, retail, food services, office buildings, television and radio stations, and research facilities throughout the state of Florida. In addition, the company has a division dedicated to facilities management for buildings located throughout the United States.

Smith has served in many civic capacities in both her local community and at the state level. She has received a number of regional and national awards for her entrepreneurial success, including Small Business of the Year and Woman of the Year for Tampa Bay as well as being listed in *Working*

Woman magazine's "Top 500 Woman-Owned Businesses." In addition, she speaks to a number of different organizations around the county about entrepreneurial business ventures.

This particular year, how did the industry panels make their choices by the lunchtime deadline? "In the judging, the cream rises to the top," explains one judge. "As a result, we generally delve unanimously into only 20 percent of the eligible companies." Judges who sit on panels assessing entrepreneurs in specific industries have specialized knowledge in that field and can evaluate candidates in the context of their particular marketplace and in relation to each other. Aside from that specialized input, however, the discussions on the industry panels are similar in content and dynamics to the discussions that occur when the chairs of each industry panel convene after lunch to select the overall national winner. All industry category winners are eligible.

Making the final decision is a formidable challenge; judges must select a single entrepreneur from the remarkable industry victors. During the initial phase, each judge advocates for the entrepreneur he or she helped select during industry-specific voting. These judges must present their entrepreneurs' stories in a compelling way. Often, a judge identifies some special or significant facet of that industry's nomination as he or she tries to convince the other judges to make that candidate the national winner.

But after a judge makes the case for a finalist, the other panel members ask hard questions. "As the judges pitch their companies, there is a natural competition in the advocacy roles. We have very challenging exchanges as gifted, articulate, and experienced judges champion their choices as being particularly powerful and unique," explains national panel facilitator Michael Camp, who is vice president of research at the Kauff-

man Center for Entrepreneurial Leadership. After every entrepreneur's story has been presented, the judges are asked to
name their top two or three choices. Frequently, this vote helps
narrow the discussion.

Camp recounts the 2001 national judging panel: "All but
one judge included the same company among their choices for
the top two. Of the total 14 choices made by seven judges, only
three companies' names came up time and again. The advocates for those three companies were called up to add to their
case, and another vote was taken."

When an initial vote for everyone's top two or three choices
does not work as cleanly as it did in the 2001 vote, the debate
comes alive. Eventually, a consensus emerges and former industry advocates become impartial judges as they focus on one winning company. The election is democratic, and the majority of
judges can select the Entrepreneur Of The Year, although for
the sake of unity, the judges often try to reach unanimous agreement on the final vote.

MEET THE JUDGES

"It impresses me each and every time that I'm involved in the judging—

both on a regional and on a national level—how much work goes into

it. The caliber and quality of the companies involved in the program

are just staggering, as are the judges who I get an opportunity to rub

elbows with. The judges are never shy about their opinions and that

makes for some wonderful and interesting dialogue. I have never been

in a situation where there's better give-and-take."

—JUDGE JIM MCCANN

MEET THE JUDGES

he good news is that people are learning to

embrace the operation of business, not as an evil,

but as a good, worthwhile, and appropriate endeavor.

—*JIM MCCANN, CEO of 1-800-Flowers.com*

Jim McCann was among the first to recognize the enormous potential in providing on-the-go consumers with quality, gift-giving opportunities. He pushed traditional boundaries to create not just one but several access channels. Today, customers of 1-800-Flowers.com can send a wide variety of floral products and gifts around the block or around the world by clicking a mouse on a personal computer, walking into one of its stores, or dialing an 800 number.

McCann has been in the floral industry since 1976, when he began building a chain of retail flower shops in the New York metropolitan area. He acquired the 1-800-Flowers phone number and renamed the company in 1986. Using a thorough understanding of his customer base and market, McCann focused on creating a reliable brand name and instilling a sense of trust and convenience in an industry that previously had had no leader. He put his company online in 1992 and in 1995 started one of the best-known retail Web sites.

McCann is a member of the board of directors of Gateway Computer, the National Retail Federation, Boyd's Bears, and Very Special Arts, as well as the boards of Hofstra University and Winthrop University Hospital. He has received numerous honors, including Retailer of the Year from *Chain Store Age Executive* magazine and Direct Marketer of the Year from Direct Marketing Day New York. His most recent book, *Celebrations,* was published in November 2001.

MEET THE JUDGES

If you train people in financial literacy, you give them a system for organizing, processing, and exercising ideas. They learn what they need to do to study a market and the competition and what they need to do to figure out where money is going to come from and how they're going to invest that money. It's a vital first step to creating innovation.

—**JOHN P. (JACK) STACK,** *President and CEO of SRC Holdings Corporation (SRC)*

Stack led the rescue of SRC when he and other employees bought it from International Harvester in 1983. Over the years, he has diversified the SRC business so that it is now a holding corporation for a number of businesses that remanufacture engines and their components, distribute engine build kits, and manufacture power units, generators, starters, alternators, and electrical components.

During his time as president and CEO of SRC, Stack authored several books, including *The Great Game of Business,* which was based on his experience implementing open-book management and teaching his workforce to be financially literate. He adapted his book into a seminar and training program, which is another of SRC's businesses. *The Great Game of Business* program has been so successful that Stack's employees have been covered by the CBS program *Eye on America* and PBS's *MacNeil-Lehrer Report.*

SRC has been selected as one of the "Top 100 Companies to Work For in America" and has received both the National Business Ethics Award and the Business Enterprise Trust Award.

Stack's next book, *A Stake in the Outcome,* provides first hand experience in using equity-sharing, stock options, and employee stock ownership to "build a business of business people." Stack is the recipient of many other business awards and honors, such as the 2000 Springfieldian of the Year by the Springfield Chamber of Commerce, an annual honor that is bestowed on a local community member who has worked to improve the quality of life in Springfield, Missouri.

EOY judges provide a unique and valuable perspective. As the founder-leaders of outstanding companies, they have "walked the talk," although for this book they've been asked to "talk the walk"—to provide their personal insights into the judging and what it means for your company.

Entrepreneur Of The Year judges have specific high standards that stem from inside knowledge. Most judges have been through the scrutiny of the judging process as candidates. More important, they have launched and managed successful businesses. They know how to evaluate nominees' accomplishments, characters, and companies. As judges, they are also standard-bearers for the Entrepreneur Of The Year, a status that denotes hard work and zealous determination.

Facilitator Ray Smilor, now president of the Beyster Institute for Entrepreneurial Employee Ownership, explains: "The judges take the process of singling out fellow entrepreneurs very seriously. They want to represent the best in entrepreneurship." One judge says her fellow EOY judges are particularly tough and have high standards because they are personally interested in maintaining and promoting the integrity of the EOY program.

Judges often mention the privilege of honoring outstanding entrepreneurs, the benefits of learning about exemplary company leaders, and the excitement of debating world-class business thinkers and doers. And, they add, being a judge is fun.

Reviewing the nominees' dossiers is "incredible . . . like getting an MBA every year," says Jack Stack, president and CEO of

SRC Holdings Corporation, a 1990 regional Entrepreneur Of The Year and a national award finalist.

"We all live in a vacuum," contends Call Solutions™ CEO George Dalton, a 1997 national finalist and a 1988 regional Entrepreneur Of The Year. Judging gives him the chance to "lift my head" and see what's going on in other companies and industries. Best of all, he says, the EOY contenders and their companies are "superior" performers.

Each judging panel includes a facilitator and judges whose empirical and academic knowledge run the gamut of business expertise. The most recent national judging panels have included facilitators such as Michael Camp, vice president of research at the Kauffman Center for Entrepreneurial Leadership and venture capitalists Kathy Behrens and Carl Thoma. The mix of judicial talent from different industries and disciplines ensures that candidates are analyzed from every possible angle.

In addition, each judge brings his or her own values to the table. As a result, judges' priorities and contributions vary widely. "It's intriguing to see the judges throw out their opinions and their different interpretations," says William H. Saito, president and CEO of I/O Software (1998 National Young Entrepreneur Of The Year and 1998 Inland Empire regional EOY). " I come from a technology background, so I have a handle on what is really new and what is just a rehash of technology. Those who come from a manufacturing or construction background tend to see things in terms of the size of the problem. Business services types look at management style."

George Dalton jokes that the range of values the judges bring to the table is one of the great things about the judging process but also one of the most frustrating. Dalton says he's a stickler about sustained performance, though when he's judging younger companies, history doesn't yet demonstrate repeated financial success or corporate longevity. In those cases, he examines the entrepreneurs' individual past performance and their other interests and patterns.

Each judge tends to prioritize a different key factor. If one pays heightened attention to bootstrap entrepreneurs, another might favor the person who swoops in to rescue an existing business. One judge may emphasize specific indicators of financial success, whereas another could demand proof of sustained performance. Such diversity among the judges enriches the conversation and provokes deeper, but not always more decisive, levels of thinking and analysis. But when the judges ultimately reach a consensus that one candidate best exemplifies excellence, they are pointing to an entrepreneur like you.

WHO ARE THE ENTREPRENEURS?

Entrepreneur Of The Year winners are your colleagues and peers. Their stories are as numerous as they are, but you can usually find something to identify with in each saga.

For example, one regional EOY winner became an entrepreneur under economic duress because he couldn't get a job. He struggled to build a software development business and, in the end, built one of the top 20 brands in the field. Another winner began a business with $300, a rundown PC, and office space in his son's bedroom. After five years, he sold his company for more than half a billion dollars. Even if you start small, there is no limit how far you can go.

Certainly, big companies contribute critical jobs and income. But in the United States, for example, Fortune 500 firms employ less than 9 percent of the workforce. Daniel Pink, author of *Free Agent Nation* and publisher of the Web site <www .freeagentnation.com>, estimates conservatively that about 33 million people in the country work for themselves—the equivalent of one of every five U.S. workers.

David Birch of Cognetics, Inc., calls dynamic, productive entrepreneurial companies "gazelles," which he identifies as firms with more than 50 employees that are growing more than 20 percent a year. Using Birch's term, Ray Smilor wrote in his book *Daring Visionaries* that "a smaller percentage [of Birch's gazelles], including Microsoft and Dell Computer Corporation, are growing faster . . . than the Fortune 500," and they are shaping a very different future.

Most Entrepreneur Of The Year winners fit Smilor's definition of "growth entrepreneurs"—those with the ability and the desire to grow as fast as possible. These distinguished entrepreneurs have succeeded in the face of rapidly changing times and have met the highest standards along the way in the areas covered in the following chapters: leadership, team building, innovation, and finance.

With this background and the information in upcoming chapters, you can use the six keys, the judges' analyses, and the entrepreneurs' achievements as a reflecting pond that mirrors your business, your goals, and the way you work. Take a close look, or better yet, come on in. The water's fine.

CHAPTER 2

Leadership

MAKE IT SO

"Leadership requires common sense, intuition, the ability to see everything, and make all the pieces fit together. It is that ability to anticipate the future and to know how to deal with it. Add the ability to articulate what they're going to do and a knack for gathering high-quality people around them to get things done, and that's a leader."

—JUDGE CARL THOMA

"Leadership means that you know how to assemble a management team and then create a culture that gets everybody working together to execute . . . new, original ideas in a way that will give you strong financial performance," explains Entrepreneur Of The Year judge Carl Thoma, practically encapsulating the scope of the six keys in a single sentence.

The judges' precise evaluation guideline for assessing leadership states: "The entrepreneurs have a vision to which they are committed, are calculated risk-takers, and personally grow as their companies grow."

MEET THE JUDGES

The Entrepreneur Of The Year Award rewards entrepreneurialism, puts examples out there, and highlights successful companies. You can't promote entrepreneurialism if the winner from two years ago is now out of business. We have to apply our wisdom to make sure an entrepreneur's success at leadership, financial stability and performance, culture, et cetera, is sustainable or enduring.

—**CARL D. THOMA**, *Managing Partner of Thoma Cressey Equity Partners*

Carl Thoma is a former Chairman and President of the National Venture Capital Association. He is the Managing Partner of Thoma Cressey Equity Partners, a private equity investment firm which he founded in 1980.

Thoma Cressey Equity Partners is currently investing out of its seventh fund, totaling $550 million. As acknowledged by *Business Week, Fortune,* and *The Wall Street Journal,* Carl has distinguished himself as a leading private equity investor in consolidating fragmented industries. Notable companies which Carl personally helped cofound include Global Imaging (third largest fully integrated office equipment distribution in the United States), National Equipment Services (fourth largest industrial and construction rental equipment company) and American Income and Life Company, which, in the early 1990s, was sold to Torchmark for nearly $600 million.

Michael Camp, a facilitator during the Entrepreneur Of The Year judging roundtables, explains that the judges ask tough questions to identify leadership in action:

- Is the entrepreneur the senior decision maker?

- Has the entrepreneur set and communicated a clear vision?

- Is the entrepreneur able to rally resources, such as a strong team and solid financial management?

- Does the entrepreneur align operations to a solid value system that warrants a national recognition?

Facilitator Ray Smilor also asks:

- How well does the entrepreneur build and use networks?

- Has the entrepreneur identified the company's key success indicators and tracked them for effective management?

- Is the entrepreneur a hands-on leader who took the company from start-up to successful, sustained operations?

- Has the entrepreneur grown as a person as the company has grown?

- Has the entrepreneur made wise decisions over time about letting go and delegating where appropriate?

- Is the entrepreneur focused on vision and values?

Whatever the particulars of their journey, successful entrepreneurs are driven by a vision and the challenge of figuring out how to get there. They have a knack for creating lasting businesses from scratch, something out of nothing. And they don't get anywhere being followers. Entrepreneurs are leaders, and how they lead makes all the difference in whether they succeed big or at all. As the judges review their criteria, they consistently identify four building blocks of leadership:

- Vision

- Passion

- Commitment

- Risk Taking

The Entrepreneur Of The Year judges perceive vision as a powerful fulcrum for moving a company forward. They are accustomed to reviewing companies where a vision seized an entrepreneur's heart and mind and reshaped that entrepreneur's professional life. In fact, facilitator Ray Smilor quotes George Bernard Shaw's description of an entrepreneur's vision as a "mighty purpose," something so significant that it becomes the entrepreneur's driving force, the motivation for becoming a leader.

People who balk at words like *vision* and *passion* think the terms are too ephemeral or intangible. But like the words *commitment* and *risk taking,* vision and passion can be observed in the real world of work. The EOY judges are especially qualified to spot the signs because they have made their visions into reality.

As an entrepreneur, you must believe in something so firmly that you are willing to do whatever is necessary to see it through. Entrepreneurial leadership, therefore, begins with a vision.

"You can see it in their eyes. You can see it in their confidence. You can see it in the way they talk."

—JUDGE JACK STACK

VISION: SEEING IS BELIEVING

A vision is an idea that an entrepreneur presents to the world in anticipation that people—fellow managers, employees, customers—will greet it eagerly. A vision can begin with a sudden awakening, a "Eureka!" moment, or it can evolve slowly over time, emerging as the entrepreneur's subconscious connects the dots of knowledge and experience. Vision is the spark that ignites entrepreneurs and inspires them to take up the baton of leadership.

Business literature is filled with attempts to define leadership. But leadership is more than just personality. It includes people's behavior and reactions, their instincts and abilities. As a result, ordinary businesspeople don't stand a chance against those entrepreneurs who have made themselves into true leaders; possess the skill to attract and empower a strong management team; communicate and exemplify a vision and a value system; overcome obstacles; and, of course, make a profit.

Often, an entrepreneur's vision springs from values he or she already holds dear. Scott Kriens already believed in the power of the global Internet—the ability of information technology to serve as a worldwide language—when he began Juniper Networks. Kriens, now Juniper's chairman, president, and CEO, was the 2000 Entrepreneur Of The Year. He initially set out to provide the best, most innovative networking solutions to enable businesses to build and connect new communication infrastructures. According to his vision, these infrastructures would span the full spectrum of Internet communications, from public access to private networks, voice, and video. High tech is what he is doing, but connecting people so they can communicate around the globe is what he believes in—that's his vision.

Like Scott Kriens, many Entrepreneur Of The Year winners report that they began by following a dream or an idea they could envision so clearly that no amount of disappointment could discourage them. This requires focused leadership from entrepreneurs who have the passion to work purposefully to fulfill a goal based on their vision.

A PASSION FOR ACHIEVEMENT

Vision is the primary tool that guides passion, providing a set of values, a sense of overall purpose, a concept of the future, and a set of long-term goals, according to James R. Lucas, author of *The Passionate Organization.* The process of creating a unified vision helps an organization fulfill the need for alignment. To create this organizational alignment, the vision must be clear, compelling, and "grown from the bottom and nurtured from the top" of the organization. A leader must ensure that the members of the organization consent to the vision and support it, and that the vision is ingrained through consistent communication. This unifying vision should be the underlying reason behind every decision.

"The passionate organization—which can exist only when composed exclusively of passionate people focused on a common vision—can alone bring the breakthroughs, the continuous improvement, the creativity and the innovation to succeed," Lucas writes.

When Entrepreneur Of The Year judges describe what it takes to win, discussion of vision is always followed closely—often in the same sentence—with discussion of the passion it takes to actualize a vision. Part of what makes an exceptional leader, judges say, is the ability to lasso passion, take it in a concrete direction, and use it to inspire others.

The 2001 National Manufacturing Entrepreneur Of The Year, James M. Bernhard, Jr., president and CEO of The Shaw Group Inc., advises: "You need to get your team to buy in and be as enthusiastic as you are about the possibilities."

Judge William Mays identifies passion as the drive that separates the entrepreneurial leader from the "supersuccessful manager/CEO."

Judge Rebecca Smith agrees: "I think the real defining issue between an entrepreneur and a manager is solely passion." She adds that "if you have passion for what you're doing [it gives you] almost a superhuman ability to continue to conquer in the face of certain defeat. So if you are doing and pursuing, everything falls into place."

Smith's tone is echoed by fellow judge Kathy Behrens, who sees entrepreneurs as people who are "consumed by passion" and who therefore "will not take no for an answer."

Being an entrepreneur requires extreme determination and the willingness to make personal sacrifices, say Joseph and Jimmie Boyett, authors of *The Guru Guide to Entrepreneurship*. They quote cookie entrepreneur Debbi Fields, who explains that you must believe passionately in your idea, even in the face of negative thinking and ridicule. But have fun with your idea, because you have to enjoy your work to remain committed to it.

Real entrepreneurship has a few key requirements, say the authors. You must feel truly passionate about your chosen field, and you must be prepared to put in long hours of work. You have to be willing to make leaps but be cautious, too, and you have to be a natural leader who is flexible and adaptable.

But most of all, you must be very excited about developing a new company. That's the passion you need to take a dream and transform it into a viable business.

Judge Kathy Behrens echoes that lesson: "You need this driven, able-to-leap-tall-buildings-in-a-single-bound characteristic to ignite and fuel a company in its early stages."

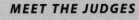

MEET THE JUDGES

What I like about the Entrepreneur Of The Year Award is that it represents a great effort to make entrepreneurialism visible. I think that's important. Entrepreneurialism is under-recognized. The award promotes the concept and rewards people for it.

—**M. KATHLEEN BEHRENS, PH.D.**, *Managing Director, Medical Technology, Robertson Stephens Investments Management*

Kathleen Behrens was a director of the National Venture Capital Association (NVCA) from 1993 to 2000 and president of the NVCA from May 1998 through April 1999. After her term as president, Behrens served as both chairman and past chairman. She currently serves as a member of the President's Council of Advisors on Science and Technology (PCAST).

Kathleen Behrens joined Robertson Stephens & Company's medical group in 1983, becoming a general partner in 1986 and a managing director in January 1993. As Robertson Stephens's first biotechnology analyst, she expanded the firm's health care presence by moving into emerging medical technologies. After nine years in research, Behrens joined the venture capital group in 1988 and has since founded several biotechnology companies, including Protein Design Labs, Inc., and COR Therapeutics, Inc. She has been instrumental in raising over $1 billion in the public and private markets for biotechnology companies. Behrens stayed with the money management group RS Investments when it bought itself out of Bank of America in March 1999.

Behrens is a director of Abgenix, Inc., and HealthTrio and represents the interests of RS Investments in GPC Biotech AG and EXACT Sciences Corporation. In addition, she held a board seat at Protein Design Labs, Inc., from 1986 to 1992; at Cell Genesys, Inc., from 1990 to 1996; at InSite Vision, Inc., from 1990 to 1995; and at COR Therapeutics, Inc., from 1988 to 1995.

Before joining Robertson Stephens, Behrens was a biotechnology analyst at Sutro & Co., Inc. She also performed genetic research for six years at the University of California, Davis where she earned a Ph.D. in microbiology.

Fellow judge Jack Stack adds that "the challenge for entrepreneurs is to get people to follow their big idea, whether it's the investment community or the people inside the organization. When entrepreneurs are able to sell their ideas, they become leaders."

Judge Steve Papermaster is often invited to speak to university classes on entrepreneurship. Usually, he starts by asking for those who see themselves as entrepreneurs to raise their hands. Most students hold up their hands because either they are entrepreneurs, at least in their own eyes, or they want to be. Papermaster startles the students sometimes when he tells them that as far as he is concerned, real entrepreneurs couldn't possibly be present in a classroom. "I realize that I am being overly dramatic," he says, "but there's a lot of truth to it. Most of what you want to learn can't be taught in a classroom. You can't teach fire; you can't teach passion."

Entrepreneur Of The Year judges say that the passion they find in entrepreneurs comes from loving what they do. Entrepreneurs need to work harder than most people, and they face many obstacles and setbacks. They may be alone in the pursuit of their passion for a long time. Many people they meet aren't convinced of the value of their vision. To keep going, entrepreneurs must not only believe in what they are doing but they must love it. Or in the words of catalogue entrepreneur Lillian Vernon, "To succeed, you must feel passionate about the work you have chosen."

ADMINISTAFF

Paul J. Sarvadi, 2001 National Services Industry Entrepreneur Of The Year and president and CEO of Administaff, is a leader with a continuing passion for his business. Like many EOY winners, he started out thinking big. He didn't question how large his company would become—he just focused on getting there. Sarvadi explains that from the very beginning he envisioned establishing a new industry, a professional employer organization (PEO). Until he started Administaff in 1986, the PEO industry had only a minor presence. Sarvadi envisioned providing human resources on an outsourced basis, and by 2000 his company was number 448 on the Fortune 500 list.

In addition, Administaff is included on Fortune magazine's list of "America's Most Admired Companies," ranks in *Forbes* magazine's "Platinum 400" of the best big companies in the United States, and appears on *InformationWeek's* list of 500 leading information technology innovators.

Today, according to its Web site, Administaff is the leading professional employer organization in the United States, serving as a full-service human resources department for thousands of small and medium-sized businesses nationwide.

Administaff's mission, which continues to reflect Paul Sarvadi's vision, is to "be the recognized leader in the development, sale and delivery of quality Professional Employer Organization services to our strategically selected market of small to medium-sized businesses. This mission will be accomplished by a highly motivated team of innovative people dedicated to finding, attracting and satisfying clients in a manner that will produce consistent and superior productivity among clients, employees and the Company."

Sarvadi's message to the public, via the Web, is clear. He writes: "As the nation's leading Professional Employer Organization, Administaff has been helping businesses get down to business for more than 15 years. We're proud to provide high-performance human resources solutions and administrative relief for busy business owners who want to spend more time building a business and less time with the employer obligations of running that business. . . . Many businesses depend on Administaff to help them succeed. We're committed to bringing you high-quality service and competitive advantages, so you can focus on your core business goals and needs."

One of Administaff's cofounders, Sarvadi is a recognized leader in shaping the development of the PEO industry. His extensive business experience, coupled with his understanding of the benefits and advantages of coemployment, make him an authority in the field. Sarvadi currently serves on the Past Presidents' Council of the board of directors of the National Association of Professional Employer Organizations (NAPEO), and he served as president of the NAPEO board of directors from 1995 to 1996. He was also one of the founders of the Texas chapter of the National Staff Leasing Association (NSLA) and served as the president of the chapter for three years. Sarvadi, who attended Rice University and the University of Houston, serves his local community in Houston as a member of the board of the DePelchin Children's Center.

The Administraff Web site proudly introduces the entire management and leadership team, which is made up of people with strong professional achievements, many of whom have been with Administaff many years.

The company provides clients with benefits and payroll processing, employer liability management, training, and evaluation, and a host of other human resource department functions. Administaff's Personnel Management System provides a comprehensive range of services, including benefits management, government compliance, employment administration, employer liability management, recruiting and selection, performance management, training and development, and owner support. In addition, Administaff's e-business strategy provides client companies and worksite employees with online information and assistance around the clock from any computer.

From its corporate offices in Houston, Texas, Administaff serves more than 4,000 clients and 70,000 worksite employees nationwide through four regional service centers and more than 30 United States sales offices. In 2001, the company had revenues of $4.4 billion and is the only PEO traded on the New York Stock Exchange.

When Paul Sarvadi was named the National Service Industry Entrepreneur Of The Year in 2001, he explained that, in his experience, companies grow more quickly when they focus on what they do best. And, he says, his company can handle the rest.

"You can read it all over their faces . . . but they don't wear it on their sleeves. They've got that intense, hungry passion, a look as though they're thinking 100 miles an hour or playing chess in their minds with lightning moves."

—JUDGE STEVE PAPERMASTER

Entrepreneur Of The Year judges use different measurements to determine if the entrepreneurs they evaluate are passionate about their work and if they are translating their passion effectively into outstanding leadership. For example, these are the measures used by three of the judges.

- Rebecca Smith: People with a passion for what they do have the energy to put in long hours and the will to structure their lives around the priorities of their business without considering that to be a sacrifice. In other words, hard work is simply part of the challenge. "If you have passion for what you're doing, your energy, innovation, and opportunities are boundless," she says.

*E*ntrepreneurial leadership is much more a blend of intuition, instinct, passion; the ability to see beyond the curve; the ability to act on conviction; the ability to maintain integrity; the willingness to take a stand, usually far in advance of any normal evidence of its being either acceptable or correct.

—**STEVE PAPERMASTER**, *Chairman of Powershift Group*

Steve Papermaster is a career entrepreneur. At age 16, he started a chain of Coney Island hot dog stands on the Galveston Island beaches; in his late teens he converted Volkswagen frames into gull-wing cars and sold them to sailors; and then he went on to start several technology ventures.

Today, Papermaster is chairman of Powershift Group, an Austin, Texas–based technology venture development company focused on building software and technology companies. He currently serves on the boards of directors for several public and private companies, including Perficient, Inc., and Vignette Corporation.

Before founding Powershift Group, Papermaster was the founder, chairman, and CEO of Business Systems Group Corporation (BSG), a global software and systems integration company. BSG was acquired by Per Se Technologies in 1996 for over $350 million.

In 2001, President George W. Bush appointed Papermaster as a member of the President's Council of Advisors in Science & Technology (PCAST). In this capacity, he serves as chairman of the Energy Independence and Innovation Committee, as well as being a member of the Technology for Combating Terrorism Committee. He is also founder and chairman of Technology Network Texas (TechNet), a national high-technology advocacy group for policy issues, and is a member of the National Executive Committee.

Papermaster received the 1996 Ernst & Young Entrepreneur Of The Year Award in Austin and has served as a national and world judge for the

Entrepreneur Of The Year Awards since 1997. In 2001, he served as the U.S. judge for the World Entrepreneur Of The Year Award. Papermaster is active as a community leader with organizations such as the American Cancer Society, the Juvenile Diabetes Research Foundation, the Jewish Community Center, and the 360 Summit.

- George Dalton: "Passion is revealed when a person is not afraid to fail."

- Kathy Behrens: Entrepreneurs are "very dedicated to their concept, driven, and passionate about their interest. They are so passionate that they're willing to fight and drive hard and overcome people and cultures that are maybe too narrow and stodgy."

Bringing their own experiences to bear, judges understand that entrepreneurs often face obstacles and detractors, especially when the odds seem stacked against them.

Judge Smith makes a distinction between a *desire* to succeed and a *passion* to succeed. She explains: "A desire is 'I want to be an entrepreneur; I want to be wealthy; I want to be my own boss.' These things don't drive you to success. They don't have enough fuel to carry you through. Passion drives you to achieve goals. In my case, I really wanted to own and operate a construction company. I wanted to do it my way, deliver [services] in a way that is different from someone else. So I had to be an innovator."

Smith's construction company, A.D. Morgan Corporation, has grown significantly each year because she had vision and passion, but she also had commitment—the persistence to hang in when even passion flagged.

COMMITMENT: IT'S THE REAL THING

Commitment is stamina, the determination to stay the course and lead people by example through adversity. It is hard work. It is faith tested. Commitment is passion and vision after the excitement wears off; commitment is a long marriage, not a hot date; a year of staying up nights with a croupy baby, not a quick tickle under a cherub's chin.

Of course, sticking it out through the difficult times is a sure sign of commitment. Judge Steve Papermaster warns that any entrepreneur's commitment is going to be tested. The way to spot winners, he says, is to look for entrepreneurs who view obstacles as interruptions on the road to success. He warns that most entrepreneurs quickly buck heads with conventional wisdom; and he tallies a laundry list of opinions that skeptics love to trot out whenever an entrepreneur begins a new venture:

- "It's not worth the risk."
- "Others have already done it."
- "It will take more resources than you have."
- "You'll never raise the money."
- "You have a nice safe job as an assistant vice president."
- "Your timing is all wrong."
- "You don't have the right people."
- "It's not worth doing."
- "You'll look ridiculous."

Well, you might check out the risk and the resources, but commitment is the key ingredient in countering the "nattering nabobs of negativity," as United States Vice President Spiro Agnew once called the nay-saying Washington press corps. Commitment counters negativity and helps entrepreneurs trust their own judgment and stay on course.

Judge William Saito equates commitment with persistence and perseverance. A committed entrepreneur will keep plugging away, he says, and won't give up even when times are stressful.

Our first book about EOY winners was titled *What's Luck Got to Do With It?* (John Wiley & Sons, 1997). Although the winners profiled for that book often spoke of luck, the real message was that luck isn't guaranteed, isn't nearly enough, and doesn't work alone. Work itself is effective. Determination is effective. Luck is a butterfly that will come and sit on your shoulder from time to time if you are fortunate, but commitment is a loyal friend who will always be there to help.

> *"Concerning all acts of initiative (and creation) there is one elementary truth, the ignorance that kills countless ideas and splendid plans: that the moment one definitely commits oneself, then Providence moves, too. All sorts of things occur to help one that would never otherwise have occurred. A whole stream of events issues from the decision, raising in one's favor all manner of unforeseen incidents and meetings and material assistance, which no man could have dreamed would have come his way. I have learned a deep respect for one of Goethe's couplets: 'Whatever you can do, or dream you can, begin it. Boldness has genius, power, and magic in it.'"*
>
> —***M.H. LAWRENCE***, The Scottish Himalayan Expedition

RISK TAKING AND TRIUMPH

Entrepreneurs are usually driven by a vision they cherish passionately. They can see the goal in the distance, but the hills are high and the way is hard. When you start a new business, you are—make no mistake about it—doing a very difficult thing. That doesn't mean you shouldn't take the risk, but you should understand it very well.

The cost of doing this is always high. Being an entrepreneur is a big risk; that's the price you pay for a shot at realizing your dream, being your own boss, or trying to become more prosperous.

Entrepreneurs spend an incredible amount of energy, time, and money being evangelists for their fledgling companies, particularly when they are trying to change consumers' preset ideas or behaviors. Then, over time, customers begin to depend on you. Employees and suppliers expect you to pay them steadily. If you fail, they lose their supply lines or their jobs, and you may lose all you invested, including your time, your savings, and your professional reputation. The phrase "bet the farm" has a base in reality. Sometimes you lose the farm. That's the risk you take.

But not every mistake means failure, and not every failure means the end of the entrepreneurial road. When entrepreneurs challenge convention, which they almost always do, they risk being wrong—but they also risk being right.

Although the methods that businesses use to overcome obstacles are discussed in detail in the chapter on change and innovation, you should know from the beginning that many entrepreneurs do bounce back from disaster, and they are wiser for the experience. After all, "if you're going to be in business, you're going to make mistakes," according to Entrepreneur Of The Year judge William Mays. "You try to avoid the catastrophic ones and you learn."

Tom Peters, author of the landmark book *In Search of Excellence*, states his advice succinctly: "Test fast, fail fast, adjust fast."

Gamblers who have made a couple of lucky guesses don't get far with Entrepreneur Of The Year judges. Facilitator Ray

Smilor explains that, instead, judges look for entrepreneurs who take calculated risks or risks for which they know the "parameters."

Not every successful entrepreneur calculates the risks or does the research, but they all eventually wish they had, even after they have survived steep learning curves.

Judge Rebecca Smith looks back on the time, 20 years ago, when she decided to enter the man's world of construction, and says, "I thought I knew it all at the time, but I didn't."

Judge Jack Stack, who took over a company that was deep in the red, explains: "There was no reason for me to be scared because I didn't know how much trouble I was really in."

Judge Robert Vukovich, who kept building his company even though he was near bankruptcy, now says, "How did I know I was going to make it? Because I was so dumb I didn't know I couldn't. Nobody told me I couldn't, so I figured, 'I'll just keep going.'" And he did.

As an entrepreneur, however, you understand that substantial up-front work and research can minimize your chance of failure. Although no amount of planning, learning, and reading will completely eliminate the possibility that something may go wrong, Entrepreneur Of The Year judges advise responsible leaders to take reasonable precautions. Judge Jeff Shuman, professor and director of entrepreneurial studies at Bentley College in Waltham, Massachusetts, says that those of you who are taking a calculated risk should go through the process of "hypothesis testing" to assess whether your calculated risk makes sense. Check it out, he says. "Test your assumptions about the business." Learn these things:

- Potential customers' needs or desires

- Potential market size

MEET THE JUDGES

f you look at why a business fails versus why one succeeds, it really comes back to the process. It matters more how entrepreneurs did it than what it is they were trying to do. They take a clean sheet of paper to figure out what needs to be done to satisfy the customers and do it profitably, and then they build that up and iterate it as they gain a better understanding of what's necessary.

—*JEFFREY SHUMAN*, Cofounder of The Rhythm of Business, Inc., and Professor and Director of Entrepreneurial Studies at Bentley College

Jeffrey Shuman, Ph.D., won an Ernst & Young Entrepreneur Of The Year Award for his outstanding achievements as a supporter of entrepreneurship. He is a professor and director of entrepreneurial studies at Bentley College in Waltham, Massachusetts. Believing that you cannot teach entrepreneurial thinking unless you practice it, Shuman has been part of the founding team of six companies in diverse industries ranging from manufacturing and distribution to software development.

Shuman cofounded The Rhythm of Business, Inc., which helps businesspeople and organizations measure and manage the value in their business relationships in order to realize strategic benefit. He and his partner, Jan Twombly, are experts in the emerging field of collaborative business. They have coauthored *Collaborative Communities: Partnering for Profit in the Networked Economy* and *Everyone Is a Customer: A Proven Method for Measuring the Value of Every Relationship in the Era of Collaborative Business*. The partners also write columns and articles that appear regularly in the *Boston Business Journal* and national trade publications and newsletters.

Bentley's Entrepreneurial Studies program is based on the iterative and intuitive business-building process first described by Shuman in his book *The*

Rhythm of Business: The Key to Building and Running Successful Companies.
Bentley's program is among the top 25 entrepreneurship programs
nationwide and among the top 4 in New England, according to the 2002 *U.S.
News & World Report* rankings.

Shuman's other honors include a Leavey Award for Excellence in
Business Education and national recognition from the Ewing Marion
Kauffman Foundation and the Coleman Foundation.

- The competitive landscape

- A plan for making money

- The cost of getting started

Ray Smilor adds these suggestions to ameliorate risk:

- Do the business research.

- Know the market.

- Get experience in the industry.

- Line up key clients.

- Analyze the competition.

Judge Jeffrey Shuman explains that entrepreneurs can
identify their key assumptions by doing their homework. Then
they can test the assumptions thoroughly with market research,
interviews, analyses, and more, which gives them a clearer picture of the risk involved.

Shuman adds that entrepreneurs often "take in new information, analyze and refine it, and then make a second set of assumptions, then a third, and so on until they clearly understand
the extent of the risk." With this depth of knowledge, an entre-

preneur can make an informed "go or no go" decision. The entrepreneur who is well armed with information can have the confidence to seek funding, build a team, assert credibility, and stand committed, a commitment based on cold, hard reality.

Once you have gained the wisdom to know if you want to persevere, you can embark on calculated risk-taking, which—like vision, passion, and commitment—is a hallmark of entrepreneurial leadership. Knowledge and information make a tremendous difference.

STRATEGY: PLANNING WITH A PURPOSE

An entrepreneur is born with vision and passion and becomes a leader by adding commitment and a willingness to understand and take calculated risks. Entrepreneur Of The Year judges face the daunting role of selecting the finest leaders from a pool of hundreds of high-caliber candidates. The entrepreneur's skill at creating and executing professional strategies is one indicator that judges rely on when assessing leadership capabilities.

A person with a vision is just another big talker with a head full of ideas until the vision is transformed into a plan, and the plan is executed. The entrepreneur must be able to take a vision and "make it so."

Not too long ago, business plans were slightly out of fashion. Newly founded Internet companies were racing to market, pushing underdeveloped products and services out the door, trying to keep up with popular demand for hotly touted technical advances that customers barely understood.

But the Entrepreneur Of The Year winners never lost their appetite for careful planning and pinpoint strategic thinking. In these times of upheaval, planning is inextricably linked to the successful pursuit of vision. However, past and present business plans are not included in Entrepreneur Of The Year nomination applications. Judges study the nominees' written statements about their entrepreneurial journeys and their future plans to assess their skill in devising and executing strategies.

In fact, judges differ in their opinions about the need for written business plans. Some judges believe that high-growth businesses change so rapidly that entrepreneurs can't maintain up-to-date written plans. Other judges, however, strongly advocate documenting your strategic planning.

"I think it's imperative," says judge Milton Grief. "If you don't have a business plan, if you don't have some kind of an idea about how you're going to take your venture forward, then you're probably operating by the seat of your pants."

Enduring entrepreneurs take a vision and turn it into a long-term strategy for business growth. Having a plan of action gives you a tool for communicating your vision, winning resources and adherents, and producing tangible results. Your business plan is a way to channel vision, passion, and commitment into a mission statement and action outline that can attract financing and energize your management team. A strong planning document is a way for you to ensure that everyone is focused on the same objectives.

Vision and passion make an important contribution to your strategic planning. James R. Lucas, author of *The Passionate Organization*, writes: "The purpose of strategy is to take our organization effectively into a better future state." At its most fundamental level, strategic planning is supposed to combine the development of overarching, long-term goals with the detailed procedures for pursuing those goals, usually accounting for a range of possible scenarios.

The issue here is that "[s]trategy is primarily concerned with synthesis: pulling together dissimilar pieces into a new and meaningful whole. But, planning is concerned with analysis:

pulling apart connected pieces into understandable components. Because people tend to elevate reason over other values," Lucas adds, "organizations often end up trying to generate a strategy from plans. Instead, organizations should develop plans from selected strategies."

And this requires aligning your strategic plan with your vision and values.

In *Finding and Keeping Great Employees,* Jim Harris and Joan Brannick maintain that strategic alignment will give your company a more consistent internal culture, a better long-range plan, and several competitive advantages, including the following:

- *Strategy.* Aligned companies meet strategic goals more easily because they can develop staffing and retention programs that maintain a motivated workforce.

- *Simplicity.* Alignment offers clear criteria for hiring, promotion, and retention.

- *Reinforcement.* People with common values make decisions that reinforce their organization's strategy and culture.

- *Company connection.* Aligned companies connect to their employees through their common values.

- *Job connection.* Alignment helps employees see the connection between individual professional duties and the company's overall goals.

- *Personal connection.* When employees share their company's values, they perceive hard work as a means of promoting their beliefs.

- *Talent center.* When your staff can achieve peak performance without having to surmount cultural obstacles,
  you'll find it easier to maintain a pool of talent.

A well-aligned, strategic plan will also give you an edge in
seeking and securing funding, a competitive arena where you
need to give every indication of following the best practices
available.

Judge Kathy Behrens, a managing director of the venture
capital firm Robertson Stephens, says top-notch entrepreneurs
have an advantage when they seek funding. "Venture capitalists
don't finance technologies or ideas; they finance people," she
explains. Behrens relies on her professional expertise when she
is assessing an Entrepreneur Of The Year candidate's leadership capabilities. She asks herself, "If this entrepreneur had
come to me, would I have funded her?" Behrens then assesses
the candidate's personality and background and hopes to be
able to say yes to such questions as these:

- Has this entrepreneur started up more than one company and done so successfully?

- Does this entrepreneur have a broad range of experience?

- Is this entrepreneur absolutely passionate and adamant
  about the company's concept?

- Are this entrepreneur's concepts thoroughly futuristic?

- Is this entrepreneur surrounded by good people?

1-800-FLOWERS.COM

Judge Jim McCann, CEO of 1-800-Flowers.com, believes that knowing what you are doing before you start is an effective way to minimize risk. "Before you jump out of the airplane," he says, "make sure you know what your parachute looks like and how it works. In other words, get close to a business or something that's along the lines of what you'd like to do, just so you can get a flavor for what it's like. Get a part-time job or do consulting work or volunteer or serve on a board. It's part of your due diligence as you write and develop your plan. It's how you really understand what you're talking about."

Mr. McCann entered the floral business in 1976 and built a chain of 14 floral shops in the New York metropolitan area, so before he acquired the 1-800-Flowers phone number in 1986, he knew flowers and he knew business. A published author and award-winning public speaker, McCann sits on the boards of Gateway Computer and OfficeMax. He has been the chairman of the board and CEO of 1-800-Flowers.com since its inception.

1-800-Flowers went online in 1992 as the first AOL merchant, and it created the 1-800-Flowers Web site (the source of this information) in 1995, when it changed its name to 1-800-Flowers.com. The company is now an e-commerce provider of floral products, gifts (from filled baskets to candies), gourmet foods, and home and garden merchandise. Its gift product line also includes the *Plow and Hearth* catalog and Web site for home décor and garden products, and greatfood.com for gourmet items. The company has strategic online relationships with America Online, Yahoo!, MSN, and NBCi, among others, and has steadily updated its Web offerings to respond to the marketplace.

According to its Web site, 1-800-Flowers.com had net sales of $310 million for the nine months ending April 2001, which at the time reflected a net sales increase of 20 percent. The company was recently named the top gift site on the Web by ClicksGuide.com. Its Class A common stock is listed on the Nasdaq under the symbol "FLWS."

The company is active in community service and provides long-stemmed pink roses to women who participate each October in the Look Good, Feel Better program, which helps women who are undergoing breast cancer surgery or chemotherapy. The company has worked with Memorial Sloan-Kettering Cancer Center in New York and has provided companywide mammogram screening at its headquarters.

Mr. McCann is also active in community service as a member of the board of directors of Very Special Arts, Hofstra University, and Winthrop University Hospital.

"1-800-Flowers.com is committed to educating its customers about flowers in a variety of ways," according to its Web site, "including lectures and design classes at the company's stores, as well as through reference areas on the Web site." The firm also maintains a comprehensive quality assurance program, which includes ongoing blind-test orders, telephone surveys with customers and recipients, in-store and mail surveys, and customer service reports. And it gives customers a 100 percent satisfaction guarantee on all products.

"We are constantly striving to make an already excellent online gift-shopping experience even better," said McCann. " Few retailers . . . can match our proven track record in handling the heavy demand we expect this year. With the enhancements to our site, combined with the enthusiastic customer acceptance of our expanded product line, we expect to build on our reputation as our customers' 'trusted guide to gifting.'"

GETTING THE JOB DONE

You can become a better leader by practicing and developing leadership skills, because experience makes leaders better if the leaders are willing to grow and change, according to authors Richard L. Hughes, Robert C. Ginnett, and Gordon J. Curphy, in their book *Leadership: Enhancing the Lessons of Experience*. While business climates and technologies are always changing, the valuable traits that make a great leader have remained constant over time.

An entrepreneurial leader must be a good strategist, but, says judge Rebecca Smith, "You have to be more than a strategist. You have to be dynamic, because once you develop a strategy, you have to lead people to your conclusion."

Judge William Saito asks a basic question when investigating strategy: "What did this entrepreneur have to do to get this far and differentiate his company from the competition?" Saito is interested in understanding the inner intelligence of the entrepreneurs. He is seeking entrepreneurial leaders who constantly challenge themselves by revisiting their plans—always aiming higher and always expanding their vision, their passion, and their commitment. Leadership has to take those elements and make them work.

CHAPTER SUMMARY

"Leadership is the number one criteria that I look at. There has to be evidence of an ability to constantly think and act as a leader in virtually all situations, regardless of circumstances, risk, or personal exposure. What I look for is a combination of facts that signal leadership exhibited over time."

—JUDGE STEVE PAPERMASTER

Leadership is the sine qua non among the judging criteria. An Entrepreneur Of The Year must possess the four building blocks of leadership: vision, passion, commitment, and the ability to take calculated risks.

Vision is the entrepreneur's underlying assumption about the way people do—or will—think and act. A vision must be grand, accessible, and flexible. As entrepreneurs learn and their companies grow, their visions often require updating. The vision can also be influenced by technological inventions, industry shifts, or other social and environmental changes.

Passion goes hand-in-hand with vision. Entrepreneurs can use passion to communicate their vision in a compelling way. Passion attracts followers and inspires leadership. Passion keeps an entrepreneur going when conventional wisdom says, "you can't do that."

Creating a business is hard work and requires commitment. Entrepreneurs generally encounter obstacles and disappointments and must rely on their commitment to see them through. Most learn that mistakes and failures add to their knowledge base and create opportunities to try again.

No business can be built without some risk taking. Prudent entrepreneurs use intense research to minimize their risk, but still they must be willing to take the chances inherent in any new business.

Leadership is more than vision, passion, commitment, and risk taking, which do not guarantee an enduring business—although a business cannot endure without them. Leaders must be able to act, and their actions must be based on long-term strategic planning that reflects their values and aligns their company with the vision they had from the very beginning.

CHAPTER 3

Team Building

PUTTING PEOPLE FIRST

"An organization is the lengthened shadow of one man."

—RALPH WALDO EMERSON

All entrepreneurs reach a time when they realize they cannot carry the full load of their new business by themselves. They need help to turn their vision into a thriving business.

When does that time arrive? At the "get-go"—right from the start.

"Entrepreneurs can get to the first plateau with a lot of sweat equity, but to get to the big picture they really need people they can count on and delegate to," explains judge Robert Vukovich.

Judge Federico Sanchez agrees: "For companies to grow, entrepreneurs must bring in people whose experience will help move the business forward."

Building a management team, however, requires just the right mix of people, as judge Steve Papermaster, chairman of Powershift Group, warns. "Winning is not just about the entrepreneur's individual talent but about how talented a team the entrepreneur can put together."

MEET THE JUDGES

t's an unusual entrepreneur who can make the transition to an effective manager. If you look at successful companies, especially technology companies, inventors normally don't wind up running the companies. They wind up in an important position with a lot of stock and an important role, but they don't wind up as the manager.

—**ROBERT A. VUKOVICH**, *Founder, President, CEO, and Chairman of WellSpring Pharmaceutical Corporation*

Dr. Robert A. Vukovich received the Ernst & Young Entrepreneur Of The Year® Award as founder and chairman of the board for Roberts Pharmaceutical Corporation, which focused on new health care solutions through the development of specialty pharmaceuticals. Vukovich sold Roberts in 1998.

By 1999, Vukovich had founded and become chairman, president, and CEO of Wellspring Pharmaceuticals, a privately held national pharmaceutical company dedicated to the development of new products related to neonatal therapy, urology, and cardiovascular medicine.

He also is chairman and founder of Infacare Pharmaceutical Corporation, a development stage company focusing on infant and maternal care prescription drug products. Vukovich hopes to take Infacare public in 2003.

Before stepping out as an entrepreneur, Vukovich had worked for several other multinational drug companies, including Warner Lambert, Bristol-Myers Squibb, and the Revlon Health Care Group, where he developed more than 45 new prescription drugs for the U.S. and international markets.

This challenge makes Entrepreneur Of The Year judges interested in the quality of people whom entrepreneurs are able to recruit, especially for their closest circle of advisors and managers. Judge Jeffrey Shuman explains: "You really need to see the caliber of the people entrepreneurs are able to rally around the vision. So you look at the boards they have, the core management team, and the employees."

Michael Dell of Dell Computers reached out for experienced help during the critical first phase of his business. He persuaded Lee Walker to join the firm as president. Walker was almost twice Dell's age, had worked as an executive in larger businesses, and had entrepreneurial experience running his own growth companies. Working together, Dell and Walker brought the then-$60 million company through its initial public offering (IPO), one of a firm's fastest growth periods.

Dell also assembled a demanding board of directors, including Teledyne Corporation founder George Kometsky and executive Bobby Ray Inman, who hailed from a Fortune 500 company and held key positions in Washington, D.C. Today, Dell Computers is the world's largest personal computer supplier.

THE LEADERSHIP TEAM

Based on her work as a venture capitalist, Kathy Behrens observes: "Often, entrepreneurs are not experienced in a wide range of areas that are very important to managing companies and growing them."

"Unfortunately, some entrepreneurs don't recognize until it's too late that there are people out there who are smarter than they are and who are needed for success," adds judge William Saito of I/O Software.

Entrepreneur Of The Year winners are an exception; they just don't get this far if they have that flawed perspective. Those who quickly and carefully surround themselves with savvy people—building a support team with the knowledge, contacts, and integrity to be an asset to their ventures—are the strongest Entrepreneur Of The Year candidates with the best and fastest-growing companies.

This is reflected in a report on leading practices by 906 CEOs from the Entrepreneur Of The Year Academy. Their firms' leading management practices include:

- Assemble a balanced advisory board and board of directors, including both internal and external directors.

- Involve the boards heavily at strategic times.

- Assemble a balanced top management team of people, combining those who have prior experience to work together with new team members.

- Use a collaborative decision-making style with the top management team.

Of course, because EOY candidates are potential future members of the Entrepreneur Of The Year Academy, judges are careful when assessing their team building skills to be sure they uphold the standards of previous winners.

SOUNDING BOARDS

Usually, judges don't receive direct information about the members of an entrepreneur's board of directors or advisors. Even so, the judges think a great deal about how important the boards are to the entrepreneur's success.

Judge Robert Vukovich notes that "the worst thing entrepreneurs can do is think they know everything. They have to know where they can go for good advice." He adds that board members bring experience to the table and can often see the big picture without getting lost in the day-to-day detail of running the business, which can happen to the chief executive.

Judge William Mays notes: "You're going to make mistakes, but you can work to avoid it by using other experts and professionals in the field as a sounding board for major decisions, such as a change in direction or the introduction of a new product."

Facilitator Behrens explains that a strong board can help build credibility for a young or growing company. A board not only reflects the quality of adherents that the entrepreneur has won but also shows that an entrepreneur is open to criticism. According to Behrens, investors are impressed with entrepreneurs who will listen to outside recommendations instead of letting their venture be stifled by inflexibility.

When it comes to selecting a board of directors, Behrens suggests that you bring in people who provide strengths that current company insiders don't have. Judge Victoria Jackson goes a step beyond that and suggests recruiting mentors or role models, senior people "who have performed very well in the same arena, who have a passion for business, and who have a passion for spreading knowledge to someone else."

When the judges evaluate management profiles, they expect to find that members of the inner management circle complement—rather than replicate—the entrepreneur's strengths and capabilities. After all, says facilitator Behrens, "It's rare for someone to understand operations, finance, sales and marketing, and human resources—*and* be a great leader."

Judges tend to agree that members of management should have extensive experience in the company's industry or discipline. The director of Entrepreneurial Studies at Bentley College, judge Jeffrey Shuman of The Rhythm of Business, Inc., explains: "Entrepreneurs really cannot afford to have someone learn on their nickel. As best they can, they want to bring in people smarter than themselves." Similarly, judge George Dalton of Call Solutions™ advises that entrepreneurs should "hire people who are better than themselves."

Facilitator Ray Smilor believes that entrepreneurs need to cultivate the ability to tolerate strength in others and to trust other managers with the realization of their vision. Tolerating strength in others is a key issue of personal development in entrepreneurs, says Smilor, and it is indicative of team-building skills.

According to judges, EOY winners succeed because they realize early in their endeavors that they need the help of others to build high-growth and lasting companies. These entrepreneurs are humble enough, or wise enough, to create leadership teams that include people with superior knowledge and experience in specific areas of business strategy and management.

EOY judges review management team profiles and examine individual roles in light of an additional key factor: how long managers have worked together. The judges also review the roles and responsibilities assigned to members of the management team. To judge Dalton, assembling managers with a history of working together successfully at another organization bodes well for their collaboration on a new venture.

"Longevity of the management team is an important indicator that they are being well led," adds judge Victoria Jackson of Victoria Belle, Inc. In other words, if judges see high turnover among the management team, they can reasonably suspect that the entrepreneur is having trouble providing direction, letting go of the reins, fostering camaraderie, or all of the above.

Judge William Saito emphasizes another point: the business leaders of today cannot be like the autocrats of yesteryear. "These people [the members of your leadership team] are very intelligent, and you cannot patronize them," he says. "They must be treated professionally." In this light, Saito pays particular attention to the way entrepreneurs include and encourage their employees' contributions.

The concept that winning in business requires bold, smart leadership isn't new, but the characteristics that indicate successful leadership have changed over time. If the Entrepreneur Of The Year awards had been given in the early 1900s, Henry Ford probably would have been honored. But in contemporary terms, he would be viewed as a hardened autocrat who lived in constant conflict with his workers. Smart management teams in the 21st century focus on making the workplace inviting so employees feel valued.

That concept only goes so far, but no further, according to judge Jim McCann. Yes, of course, the boss shouldn't be an autocrat and should make people feel valued. But, he says, "While you want to get people's input, you have to maintain the premise that, at the end of the day, it is not a democracy. Even though five out of six people don't think a choice is a good way to go, you have to at some point make the decision you think is right for the company. It is your job to make the hard decisions."

One of the hardest decisions for you, the entrepreneur, to make is designating who will be in charge if something happens to you. What is the succession plan for your company? Who will step up to the plate and keep your business going strong?

Not every Entrepreneur Of The Year portfolio includes a succession plan, but each one should. Such a plan gives the judges another way to assess how well entrepreneurs use planning, training, and development for effective team building. Judge Victoria Jackson states strongly that "if entrepreneurs can't identify their replacements, I assume either they aren't developing their people or they have great people whom they aren't recognizing."

*O*ne thing about entrepreneurs is that they don't want to be dependent on the whims of Wall Street, the ups and downs, because to build a successful business, they really need the flexibility of not worrying about quarter-to-quarter performance. They take a longer-term outlook.

—**WILLIAM MAYS**, Founder and President of Mays Chemical Company

William Mays transformed Mays Chemical Company from a one-person operation into a company that serves clients in all 50 states, Canada, and Puerto Rico. Mays Chemical is one of the top 20 chemical distributors in North America. It is a fully integrated distributor of chemicals, related raw materials, formulated products, outsourcing services, cleaning and sanitation systems, and chemical management expertise. The company specializes in products for the food, beverage, pulp and paper, pharmaceutical, and automotive industries, among others.

Black Enterprise magazine honored Mays Chemical as Company of the Year and reports that the company's success can be tied to its "tried-and-true business strategy of diversifying the client list, servicing industries with long-term profitability, and capitalizing on opportunities to reinvest in the firm."

Mays Chemical has won numerous other awards for excellence, such as the prestigious General Motors (GM) Outstanding Supplier of the Year—given only to GM's top 1 percent of suppliers worldwide.

Judge Stack of SRC Holdings warns: "I see companies absolutely destroyed when the founding entrepreneur is gone. That means the entrepreneur and other managers didn't set up a defined process for lining up people who are able to grow the company."

Since the early years of the Entrepreneur Of The Year competition, judges have assessed the character of the nominated entrepreneurs and have examined how well the management team's skills and behaviors align with the entrepreneur's vision and values. Because an entrepreneur leads by example, the judges heed the example that is set—and the message that is sent—by the nature of the people selected to help run the business.

CREATING A CORPORATE CULTURE

The sum of people's behaviors, attitudes, and motivations—from business planning to interacting with customers, fellow employees, vendors, or business partners—is the culture of your organization. Your corporate culture is composed of the specific practices that your employees believe symbolize and represent your business.

According to judge Federico Sanchez, culture is "what makes people happy working as part of the team and makes them proud to be associated with the entrepreneur and the company."

A classic example of an extraordinary entrepreneur whose company is renowned for its culture is Herb Kelleher, retired CEO of Southwest Airlines and 1991 Master Entrepreneur Of The Year. Most of the airline industry has always floundered but not Southwest. In fact, other airlines have tried to duplicate Southwest's no-frills, point-to-point service. What competitors can't imitate, however, is the "help-each-other-out" teamwork that is intrinsic to the culture Kelleher created at Southwest.

SOUTHWEST AIRLINES

What enables a Southwest ground crew to turn planes around in one-third the time other airlines require? How does Southwest make a profit when other airlines are struggling? The answer: Southwest has developed a culture all its own.

Cofounder (with Rollin King) and Chairman of the Board Herb Kelleher, an Entrepreneur Of The Year winner, and his leadership team start with a rigorous recruiting process designed to identify high-energy, positive thinkers who have a great sense of humor. Employees go through training that emphasizes how everyone working together can keep planes in the air and customers coming back. In their book *Nuts: Southwest Airlines' Crazy Recipe for Business and Personal Success,* authors Kevin Frieberg and Jackie Frieberg credit Southwest's tremendous success to its very individualistic corporate culture.

Southwest embraced the idea of being "nuts" and gave it a positive spin. Its "go nuts" philosophy permeates the entire company. The result is a uniquely inventive, creative workplace that functions in a supportive, relaxed atmosphere conducive to innovation, say the Friebergs. For instance, in one famous episode then CEO Kelleher arm wrestled Kurt Herwald, chairman of Stevens Aviation, instead of going to court in a dispute over an advertising slogan.

Southwest prides itself on having a maverick corporate personality made up of determination, a flair for being positively outrageous, the courage to be different, the vulnerability to care and love, the creativity to be resourceful, and an esprit de corps that bonds people.

These aren't just descriptive phrases. Rather, they are qualities nurtured in every Southwest employee and sought in every new recruit, write the Friebergs. Business basics with a Southwest twist may look like it's undisciplined, but that couldn't be further from the truth. In fact, Southwest's freedom is a discipline in and of itself. Southwest has always adhered to a clearly defined purpose and a well-thought-out strategy.

Southwest Airlines reinvented air travel 30 years ago by flying (so to speak) in the face of convention; that is, doing the opposite of what is normal in corporate culture. With its low fares and fun, irreverent style, Southwest "made flying an event."

Using a creative approach on every level, the airline urged its employees to "color outside the lines." According to the Friebergs, the results validated Kelleher's philosophies and astounded the corporate world.

Southwest keeps airfares low by keeping costs low, retains customers by getting everyone and their baggage to their destinations on time, practices the Golden Rule at work and in the community, and has record-setting productivity and safety records—all while making a profit.

Today, Southwest flies 2,800 daily flights, employs 34,000 people (81 percent unionized), and serves 59 airports in 30 states, according to its customer-friendly Web site.

The airline began service in Texas on June 18, 1971, with flights to Houston, Dallas, and San Antonio. It has become the fourth largest U.S. airline (in terms of domestic customers carried). Year-end results for 2001 marked its 29th consecutive year of profitability. Southwest became a major airline in 1989 when it exceeded the billion-dollar revenue mark and is now the United States' only major short-haul, low-fare, high-frequency, point-to-point carrier. It is a member of the Fortune 500 and appears regularly on a myriad of other quality-indicator lists.

The "fun facts" on its Web site note the following:

- In 2001, Southwest reviewed 194,821 résumés and hired 6,406 new employees.

- Southwest booked 7.2 million reservations monthly in 2001.

- Southwest served 91.7 million bags of peanuts and 5.2 million bags of raisins in 2001.

- The shortest daily flight is between Long Island/Islip and Providence, R.I. (108 miles). The longest daily flight is between Providence and Phoenix (2,271 miles).

- Southwest Airlines has the shortest taxi-in time (time from landing to arriving at the gate) at 3 minutes and 40 seconds.

- Southwest received requests for service from 165 destinations in 2001.

- Southwest employs 960 married couples; in other words, 1,920 Southwest employees have spouses who also work for the company.

Its off-the-charts culture, its customer orientation, and its inclusive approach to its workforce are unique. In fact, throughout its Web site, the words *customer, employee,* and *company* are capitalized consistently. Southwest, which is known for its budget fares that average $83.99, has ranked number one in having the fewest customer complaints for the last 11 years. In May 1988, it was the first airline to win the coveted Triple Crown for a month—Best On-time Record, Best Baggage Handling, and Fewest Customer Complaints. Since then, the airline has won the crown more than 30 times. It was the first airline with a frequent-flyer program to give credit for the number of trips taken rather than the number of miles flown. Southwest also pioneered senior discounts, Fun Fares, Fun Packs, a same-day airfreight delivery service, ticketless travel, and many other innovative programs.

Southwest gives back to its destination communities by sponsoring major community and civic festivals. It promotes African American community events in more than 20 cities through national sponsorships with BET (Black Entertainment Television) and Tom Joyner. It also offers a "virtual pilot" online program that teachers can use to instruct children in math, geography, and other subjects. Its primary corporate charity is the Ronald McDonald House program, which has received more than $4.8 million over the past 16 years in proceeds from the Southwest-sponsored LUV Classic golf tournament.

The company's guidelines, as reported by the Friebergs, include the following tips that your organization can follow:

- Live within your budget.

- Manage in good times for bad times.

- Define your own targets. Don't settle for conventional standards; create your own.

- Keep things simple. Streamline your systems and your life.

- Bigger isn't always better. Don't confuse market share with profitability.

- At the peak of success, look for things you can do even better.

- Be humble: success is hardly ever all your own doing and rarely irreversible.

- Hire for attitude, train for skill.

"I want flying to be a helluva lot of fun!" Kelleher always says. "Life is too short and too hard and too serious not to be humorous about it." Fun is serious business at Southwest. King and Kelleher began with a simple notion: If you get your passengers to their destination when they want to get there, on time, at the lowest possible fares, and make darn sure they have a good time doing it, people will fly your airline. And as its Web site says, "You know what? They were right."

Like Southwest, you want to create a culture that gives all the stakeholders in your company—employees, customers, clients, shareholders, and the community—a clear sense of your company's identity.

Embracing your core culture is an important task because it sets the standard, say authors Jim Harris and Joan Brannick in their book *Finding and Keeping Great Employees.* It is also a difficult task, because it requires extreme honesty, even enough to challenge your company's mission or vision statements. You may even determine that your company's current core culture doesn't support its long-term strategic objectives. In that case, you will have to battle to realign your company's culture and its mission.

World-class entrepreneurs use their corporate culture to imbue their management teams and their initial employees with dedication to a common purpose and a common set of values and goals. Then, as ventures grow and entrepreneurs have less day-to-day contact with the majority of employees, they can trust that the team environment they have fostered will remain, much like a lengthened shadow.

To assess the culture of an organization, judges work from the premise that culture evolves from whether and how entrepreneurs communicate and if they reward the right set of principles and business goals. Judge Jim McCann cautions: "Entrepreneurs can only influence culture. They do it by selecting which things they choose to reward, which things they choose to punish, and which things they choose to celebrate."

To see your employees' point of view, judge Jeffrey Shuman cites a suggestion from Peter Drucker, who said that entrepreneurs would do well to think of their employees as volunteers. "Even . . . in a weak market, people are essentially volunteering to work for a company. They are getting paid, but they volunteer to be there," judge Shuman says. Given this mind-set, entrepreneurs quickly realize that they want to create a place where employees enjoy spending their time and where the organization's mission gives meaning to what they do. Other judges agree with judge Shuman, who notes that talented people who can meet a new venture's needs are a precious and scarce resource.

*T*here's a commonsense test, which basically means
the entrepreneur takes his idea and goes out to the potential
beneficiaries—whether they're customers or partners—and asks them to
help develop the idea. If the beneficiaries don't care enough to put more
than just a casual interest forward, then there's probably something about
the idea that ought to be revisited, because it must not be good enough.

—*SCOTT KRIENS*, Chairman, President, and CEO of Juniper Networks

Just a few months after Scott Kriens won the Ernst & Young
Entrepreneur Of The Year Award, he was hailed by *Business Week* as one of the
"Top 25 Managers to Watch."

Kriens was invited in 1996 by Juniper Networks' founders to take the
helm at the then fledgling firm, which furnishes high-performance Internet
provider (IP) network-routing solutions that service providers use for growing
the global Internet backbone. Kriens built Juniper Networks from its early
days of product development to its current broad commercial success. He
brought the company public and in its first full year as a public company
posted a profit and raised market share for Internet routers from 17 per cent
to 30 per cent. Juniper Networks is now a leading provider of core, edge,
mobile, and cable IP services and systems. Talking about his success, Kriens
says, "It's focus, not magic." Juniper Networks, he says, has never strayed from
its simple goal of just building the best Internet equipment. And it helps, says
director Vinod Khosla, who lured him to Juniper Networks, that Kriens is a
gifted strategist and team builder.

Before joining Juniper Networks, Kriens was a cofounder and officer of
StrataCom, Inc., in both operations and sales capacities from 1986 to 1996; and
he serves as a director for VeriSign, Inc., Equinix, Inc., and Calient Networks, Inc.

The right culture varies from business to business, but the judges share a standard set of expectations when evaluating Entrepreneur Of The Year candidates. The first expectation is that all employees can state their individual contribution to the fate of the business. Judge William Saito says that if he were to drop in on a business one day, he would begin deciphering the company's culture by "starting on the ground floor of the operation with the people who actually produce the product or service." He says, "They should be able to articulate what they're working on and why and how it relates to the vision."

A recent study (quoted in the essay "Tolerating Bad Leaders" by Jean Lipman-Blumen in the anthology *The Future of Leadership Today*) of 100 student leaders in top undergraduate business programs found that tomorrow's leaders must:

- Communicate an inspirational global vision

- Be technologically competent

- Employ and promote an open-minded leadership approach

- Advocate diversity

- Demonstrate respect toward employees and flexibility

- Nurture an organizational culture that emphasizes teamwork

In that vein, judge Jim McCann adds that judges want to know what an entrepreneur has done to shape an internal culture that positively affects the experience of employees and customers. He declares, "We are looking for people who are doing clever and unique things to embolden, develop, embrace, and promote the entrepreneurial spirit in their companies."

How does a company treat its staff? How does it develop its people? How does it motivate and reward them?

Overall, EOY judges say that team building stems from an entrepreneur's values and is sustained through a culture that demands effective recruiting, employee development, and incentives for excellent performance. Therefore, an entrepreneur's success at team building is demonstrated—or denied—by the company's culture.

YOUR EMPLOYEES: RECRUITING AND HIRING

"You are only as good as your people. Find and hire the best.

Don't compromise."

—BUSINESS WRITER JOHN ZENGER

Some of the toughest decisions that entrepreneurs make are in the realm of hiring (or, when necessary, firing), especially when the venture is just starting. Judge Scott Kriens of Juniper Networks says this is particularly critical with "the first 50 employees. They are so important [because they] help form the culture and buy into the vision. You build the company around them."

First hires are critical to entrepreneurs' team-building achievements. While companies grow and entrepreneurs have less daily opportunity to influence corporate culture, entrepreneurs rely on their first employees to carry on and reinforce the values, vision, and objectives on which a venture is founded. When you hire the right people, it's easier for you to delegate because you can trust their competence. These valued early employees set the company's pattern for recruiting people who are capable and trustworthy performers.

Some EOY candidate dossiers omit information about an entrepreneur's established recruiting practices. That omission makes the judges alert for information that might reveal how people come to join the firm. Entrepreneurs who follow the best practices in the field operate their recruiting function in a way that reflects their operating values and their focus on their company's objectives.

Judge Scott Kriens is clear that the recruiting process becomes smoother and the quality of people you can bring becomes much higher when you have a good idea of what to say when you recruit. "The mission the company is on, its ability to accomplish the mission, its differentiation, and the substantive reasons why the company is going to be great have to be visible and obvious to a prospective employee," he says.

When Juniper was smaller and Kriens was directly involved with every hire, he made the majority of hiring decisions based on how well the person's work matched the values he and his cofounders promoted. "Making that fit is the best way to develop the kind of culture and passion that ends up creating the entire company," explains Kriens.

Kriens's management team is so confident that they have hired the right people that they use employee referrals as their most trusted recruiting technique. Employees have referred fully 75 percent of the people Juniper has hired. "We actually have a system by which everyone who comes into the company is charged with bringing in one more equally talented person from their past experience," says Kriens, who believes that excellent employees already share the company's vision, so they are likely to know other people who will do the same.

Judges see a vast range and variety of employee recruitment, training, and development initiatives, including everything from reimbursement for degree and certificate programs to company-sponsored workshops and mentoring programs. EOY judges view employee development as a clear sign of an entrepreneur's commitment to building a company that is meant to last.

Looking at recruitment practices offers judges one way to evaluate an entrepreneur's mastery of team building. How well entrepreneurs recruit and retain an entire workforce provides another measuring stick. In a high-growth business, entrepreneurs quickly become removed from day-to-day recruiting and interaction, so it is a challenge to create a productive environment where everyone feels secure and continues to share the same business values and objectives over time.

For example, judge Jack Stack wants his employees to know, not only do they have a future with SRC Holdings, but they *are* its future. He established a unique training program that puts every employee, including the assembly line workers in his engine refurbishing plants, through courses on financial engineering and reading a balance sheet. He believes that companies perform better when leaders elevate the thinking of the people inside the organization.

"Teach people what it took to make a great and enduring company," Stack says. "Change the way business is managed by expecting employees to build a great company rather than a great product or service."

Judge Stack tells the illustrative story of a department leader who was convinced that she couldn't learn anything that would help her group improve the company. "She managed the people who make fuel injectors, so I worked with her to break out data about that function. We got all the market data, including competition and cost of materials, for all 14 parts of an injector. She even learned to understand gross margin. Afterward, I immediately saw a huge behavioral change. She began focusing on how much profit she could make on the injector, not just on how to produce it.

"She took a product line that had 27 percent margin and built it into a line with a 43 percent margin. She realized that she could save $12 for every nozzle tip that she could save rather than throw away. So she bought capital equipment to save the nozzle tips. She made an investment that more than paid for itself."

In a similar approach, judge Jim McCann asserts that "one of the real joys in my life is to see employees of mine who don't have the 'requisite pedigree' turn out to be terrific managers." One of his favorite scenarios involves women employees who have returned to the workforce after their children are old enough to go to school. "This employee might come to work part-time, and two years later she's running a big department or a division, even though she might not have gone to college or finished a degree," notes McCann. "We have dozens of those cases in our company."

On the other hand, as difficult as it is to find the right person to hire, it is just as difficult to let people go when the business outgrows them or their performance is not up to your standards. As judge Robert Vukovich says, "I don't mean to sound heartless, but you have to be able to shed individuals who are not really working in a manner consistent with your overall objectives." The best solution is to hire the right people in the first place, which is, of course, every entrepreneur's intention.

Jack Taylor and his son, Andy Taylor, of Enterprise Rent-A-Car, both believe that their recruitment of well-rounded employees is one reason they have been so successful. For example, when Enterprise recruiters visit college campuses, they don't necessarily look for the highest academic achievers. Instead, they seek people who are flexible and hard working. Rather than interview the top 10 percent of the class, Enterprise recruiters might look closely at a sorority social coordinator or a member of the basketball team.

Management must develop a set of passion-oriented recruitment and retention measures in addition to administering the usual skill and intelligence tests, advises author James R. Lucas. When you are recruiting, look for expressions of passion about your firm's values and visions, about learning and meeting challenges, about communities and other human beings, and about the kind of work the potential employee will be doing. Cultivate a learning environment that offers your employees opportunities for training and mentoring in the skills your organization values, Lucas states. Promote through the ranks and encourage experienced employees to teach and share their knowledge and wisdom. As a matter of follow-through, you should include efforts to implement these values in your company's ongoing employee evaluations.

Facilitator Ray Smilor says that in addition to setting the company's environmental tone and communicating the firm's objectives, the entrepreneur's role in team building is "reveling in the talent, skill, experience, and knowledge of others and celebrating those who bring that knowledge and skill into the company." He compares the entrepreneur to a symphony conductor who provides solo opportunities to different instrumentalists so that everyone gets a chance to shine.

But first they have to learn to play the instruments and the music—that's training. They have to practice and hone their skills—that's development. And they have to want to play—that's motivation.

RETAINING AND MOTIVATING YOUR EMPLOYEES

"Your employees are the spinal cord of your company."

—ARTHUR BLANK, Cofounder of Home Depot

Employee motivation is based on connecting your employees' interest to your organization's interest. *Motivating Employees* authors Anne Bruce and James Pepitone contend that people are naturally "motivated to do what they believe is in their best interest." But "you can't motivate other people. You can only influence what they are motivated to do." That means "your goal as a manager should be to help employees identify their welfare with that of the organization. When that happens, they will naturally feel motivated to work hard."

Motivation should be linked to self-interest but in a practical way that entrepreneurs can utilize. Whatever part external factors play in motivation, "they're always subject to our individual, intrinsic concerns—that is, we have to buy into them," the authors continue. That requires leadership that helps people feel "inspired to cooperate," which happens "when they understand how their work adds value to the organization, and when they feel empowered to make decisions about their work." You should do the following:

- "Create an environment where employees feel motivated to do a great job every day."

- To "influence people's motivations, you have to uncover their reasons for doing things, their purposes and their causes. People aren't going to be truly motivated for your reasons and goals."

- "People act according to their basic needs. Know what drives each of your employees so that you can link job activities with each individual's personal needs and help him or her find greater motivation to perform well."

- "Encourage entrepreneurial thinking because people who feel ownership of something tend to care more about it."

- "Employees today want some input into how their organization is run. They want to have influence and make a contribution."

- "Your expectations affect the behavior of your employees. If you expect better performance and trust employees to deliver, you're likely to get it."

- "When you give power to your employees, you show how much you trust them and you give them reason to trust you."

- "Show faith that your people will do the job right." (from *Motivating Employees*)

Entrepreneurs can use three basic motivational keys to provide employees with intrinsic motivation: collaboration, content, and choice, according to Bruce and Pepitone. Collaboration is critical, because people are more motivated to work hard when they want to cooperate and help others succeed. Content is essential, because people feel more inspired to work diligently when they recognize how their work adds value to the organization and contributes to their "work community." And choice is necessary because people are eager to work harder when they "feel empowered to make decisions about their work."

As an entrepreneur, help your employees think more like entrepreneurs. Your training and development program should explain the nature of the company fully and should demonstrate how it functions and makes money.

Help employees better understand the competition and encourage them to take intelligent risks. Inspire them to engage in "innovative thinking," the authors suggest. As part of this empowerment process, support your employees if they make mistakes, and treat errors as learning opportunities. You can use special training programs or brainstorming sessions to teach your employees more about the company, allow them to provide input in how it can improve, and explore their ideas. You can instill the spirit of teamwork in your people, a spirit based on a "cohesive, energizing, and compelling force that brings individuals together to work toward a common goal."

Judges explain that entrepreneurs are doubly challenged because they must find, train, motivate, and retain people who provide invaluable competencies and who also embrace the entrepreneur's vision and values. However, those common values are a key element in employee motivation.

People want to make a difference and be part of a greater whole, says author James R. Lucas in *The Passionate Organization*. You can use internal marketing and alignment techniques to make current and future goals compelling to the rank and file. When the organization does accomplish its goals, make sure to recognize that these accomplishments arise from everyone's efforts.

As judges note when they review human relations portfolios, however, praise and recognition cannot be the only elements in employee motivation. To build strong teams, real responsibility must be shared.

You should make employees collectively responsible, advises Donald L. Laurie in *The Real Work of Leaders*. You must promote shared responsibility to bring everyone together in using shared values to work toward a new purpose. Give the job and the follow-through responsibility back to those employees who can do it. Then they will have to resolve the problem. Monitor their attitudes to make sure they are willing to accept accountability and responsibility. For instance, this means that frontline employees who are working closely with customers should be alert to market changes and growth opportunities. Laurie notes that they should be willing to take the initiative and express their ideas.

You have to do more than just give employees a sense of empowerment and assume that they will feel and act empowered, he cautions. You need to help employees feel comfortable taking on this added responsibility along with giving them input into decisions regarding their work so they feel a greater sense of control over what they are doing.

Commitment is just as important on the part of an employee as it is on the part of an entrepreneur. James Lucas urges you to remain focused on the goal of motivation: To direct employees' passion toward the goals of the organization, he explains, management must understand that its goal is commitment, not loyalty. A loyal employee will always show up bodily, but committed employees direct their minds and spirits to the organization's goals.

Some Entrepreneur Of The Year nominations include results from employee satisfaction surveys. Judges, of course, use this information in their assessment of an entrepreneur's team building capabilities. The judges consider the existence of an employee satisfaction survey an indication that the entrepreneur takes team-building seriously enough to measure it and manage it.

Lucas further notes that besides inspiring motivation in each employee, entrepreneurs want to inspire employees to work together as a team. To do this, he suggests, encourage team members to do more together than any one person could accomplish alone. Show your concern for team members. Let them know you care about your work and theirs. Emphasize how people can make a difference by working together.

To be sure that employees want to continue with his company over the long term, Entrepreneur Of The Year judge Jack Stack conducts employee morale surveys twice a year. His firm's surveys include 15 questions, but judge Stack has learned that one question matters the most. "There's a question about how your supervisor treats you as a person," he says. "If we fail on that question, we fail on the whole test." Stack has incorporated the results from this survey into the company's management development process.

In an extensive 20-year study of the U.S. workplace, John Buckingham and Harold Coffman of the Gallup Organization interviewed countless employees. They have concluded that their most powerful discovery is that people leave managers, not companies. They found that "how long employees stay and how productive they are while they are employed depends on their relationship with their immediate supervisor." The Buckingham and Coffman result is surprising because it differs from long-held beliefs that a strong leader at the top and generous pay and benefits are enough to attract, motivate, and retain talented employees.

Entrepreneur Of The Year judges seem to inherently understand these workplace dynamics. Since the early years of the Entrepreneur Of The Year Awards, the judges have delved into the profiles and roles of managers and team members. The managers' tasks are important because the judges believe, as Theodore Roosevelt once said, "The best executive is one who has sense enough to pick good people to do what he wants done, and self-restraint enough to keep from meddling with them while they do it."

This attitude expressed so well by Theodore Roosevelt is part of the corporate culture at Ernst & Young, which explains on its Web site that its commercial success is accomplished "within a unique culture that puts our people first. We strive to help all of our people achieve both their professional and personal goals through an environment that fosters growth and provides continuous opportunities to develop new skills and knowledge. As a result, Ernst & Young has been included in the Fortune 100 Best Companies to Work For, a ranking of advanced, innovative companies that help employees balance work and personal life."

And this is the way that solid entrepreneurial organizations should view their "human capital," according to *The Future of Leadership*. Entrepreneurs should focus on their organization's need for knowledge and skills. The core description, then, becomes a description of the person, not the job, because it is the person filling the job that matters. The authors note that because skilled people have more employment options, advanced workers will be able to select where they work, what activities they perform, and the "company they keep." In this era, each worker must become a manager of his or her own career, so the job an employee has with your company must become more than just a job.

Organizations must learn to harness their employees' positive passions for achievement, Lucas writes. Therefore, to assess an entrepreneur's success at team building, judges examine not only the entrepreneur's leadership team but also any initiatives the entrepreneur has created and sponsored to empower, nurture, and reward the workforce.

When evaluating Entrepreneur Of The Year nominees, judges assess their corporate culture to see what it does to retain and develop its workforce. Their criteria includes questions for determining if your company offers meaningful programs and educational opportunities that reward employees who exemplify your company's values, advance your company's vision, and honor your company's responsibilities toward clients and customers.

EMPLOYEE REWARDS AND RECOGNITION

EOY judges agree that rewarding employees—above and beyond their salaries, benefits, and promotions—boosts morale and helps define your company's culture. They offer examples, such as office parties, outings, and recognition events, as simple ways entrepreneurs can reward employees for their work and celebrate their successes. Other perks, such as on-site childcare services and/or fitness facilities, can help retain workers because perks make their life more convenient and balanced, and they reinforce the company's respect and appreciation of its workers.

Judge Victoria Jackson echoes many EOY judges when she says that the greatest entrepreneurs will use creative reward programs to share profits with their employees. As judge Federico Sanchez notes, Entrepreneur Of The Year judges like to see companies offer financial rewards and encourage participation to the people who have been the most important in creating the wealth for the entrepreneur in the first place. In fact, profit sharing and equity compensation are hallmarks in many EOY-run companies.

Of course, judges also advocate tying incentives to goals that promote company values and move the company closer to realizing its vision.

Judge Jack Stack explains his formula for rewarding people: "Number one is teach people the rules. Second, have a scorecard because people really respond to goals. Third, give people a stake in the outcome."

Facilitator Carl Thoma mentions Jack Taylor and his son, Andrew, as consummate examples of entrepreneurs who "share wealth" as an incentive for superior performance. The Taylors, who were the 1997 National Entrepreneur Of The Year winners for their management of Enterprise Rent-A-Car, exemplify other valuable team-building traits, such as nurturing employees' career growth and teaching employees to be entrepreneurial.

Enterprise has been an industry leader in its treatment of customers and employees, particularly in its innovative compensation package. As an entrepreneur, you have many options in designing a compensation package that meets the needs of your employees and your company. In *Rewarding Teams: Lessons from the Trenches,* Glenn Parker, Jerry McAdams, and David Zielinski outline the six basic types of reward plans. Three of the plans specifically offer recognition and incentives for teams and the organizational unit as a whole. The six types of plans are:

1. *Compensation and benefits.* These entitlements are a cost of doing business. They focus on rewarding individuals, so you attract employees and keep the good ones.

2. *Special reward plans based on competencies.* These plans acknowledge individual contributions according to how well employees fulfill their responsibilities, share their expertise, or utilize any special business or financial competency.

3. *Individual incentives.* These incentives, which include such things as sales commissions, reward the achievement of a certain performance or result.

4. *Recognition plans.* These plans can apply to individuals, teams, or permanent work groups. Unlike an incentive, recognition follows a particular result. Most recognition plans celebrate organizational objectives, reinforce outstanding individual or team performance, recognize years of service, or reinforce desired behaviors or activities.

5. *Project team incentives.* Usually, a team's sponsor or mentor will create these incentive plans, which are generally based on achieving a specific objective. And these measures typically involve reaching a project milestone, completing a project, or adding a certain measure of value, such as reduced turnaround time on customer requests. Don't tie financial incentives to milestones, as milestones can change for good reasons, such as technological advances. Instead, use recognition after the fact.

6. *Organizational unit incentives.* These rewards cover a complete organizational unit, such as the whole company, division, or work group, and can be the most powerful of all the reward plans in supporting a culture of teamwork in your company. This approach is powerful because it involves most of your employees, pays out only when the improvement occurs, and follows results rather than activities. You can also change the incentive as the needs of your business change. In addition, the incentives make managers at all levels accountable for the accomplishments of the people in their area of responsibility.

You should consider using a mix of reward plans based on the needs of your business, say the authors of *Rewarding Teams.* Whatever plan you choose, its effective implementation depends on:

- Gaining management ownership at all levels

- Rolling out the plan and operating it as a business strategy, including telling employees what you are measuring and regularly getting their feedback about the plan

- Assessing the effectiveness of the plan, generally through a quarterly performance review, and making adjustments as necessary

"Most basic compensation and benefit plans should be viewed as nothing more than entitlements—a cost of doing business, a part of the employment agreement between employee and employer," the book notes. "They focus on the individual, and their objective is to attract and, with luck, retain employees."

Entrepreneur Of The Year judges teach that the challenge of holding on to good people and inspiring them to be effective comes with your success in attracting and hiring the right people in the first place. As judge Vukovich explains, team building "is a matter of learning how to make people work in a competitive environment, stimulating them to keep them happy, and keeping them motivated so that everybody's pulling the oars at the right time, and the boat goes in the right direction."

Judge Saito warns that without teamwork a company is sure to experience "the Dilbert effect. People may think they're working under a single vision, but they're veering off a couple of degrees here, a couple of degrees there. It's extremely inefficient and difficult to get everything back on track."

However, strong entrepreneurs know, in the words of authors Harris and Brannick, that "[a] driving force behind today's disconnection is that today's employees are searching for something more than just a paycheck from their work.

"Employees need to feel connected to something more permanent and enabling than a company logo or a job title."

In the end, according to Douglas L. Laurie, author of *The Real Work of Leaders,* "In business, the primary mission of the . . . leader is to mobilize people . . . to engage in their work."

YOUR STAKEHOLDERS

Often, the most profitable companies are those that create jobs in the local economy, treat their employees very well, develop innovative products and services, take care of the environment, and contribute positively to the community—in other words, they heed their stakeholders' interests, as Ann Svendson notes in *The Stakeholder Strategy*.

Business leaders and managers can establish, maintain, and benefit from various kinds of mutually beneficial, collaborative stakeholder relationships. Stakeholders are your company's employees, shareholders, suppliers, colleagues, customers, and communities, Svendon says. Companies that proactively respond to their shareholders' interests actually do better than those that buffer themselves from any outside influence.

Author James R. Lucas agrees, noting: "Having established a passion-friendly environment through vision and mutual trust, build passion for stakeholders, including customers, investors and 'helpers,' such as vendors and service providers, through the development of each individual's natural empathy."

Entrepreneurs need to learn as much as possible about their stakeholders' needs and consider the impact on them when making decisions. Then make the stakeholders "visible" to your employees and equip employees with the organizational knowledge to interact with them "helpfully and appropriately."

CUSTOMER SERVICE

An excellent corporate culture is customer focused. Assessing how your employees prioritize your customers is a litmus test for judge Steve Papermaster, who wants to know, "What do your employees talk about and what do they spend their time on? How do they treat customers and prospects?"

Marketing expert Philip Kotler says entrepreneurs should "seek to get all their departments to be customer-oriented, if not customer-driven."

You can find out if your customers are satisfied—if they think your business exists to fill their needs. Just ask them. John H. Zenger, author of *22 Management Secrets to Achieve More with Less,* asks entrepreneurs several questions:

- Do you know how your customers feel about your business?

- How do they rate your business compared to your competitors?

- Do they think your product or service is improving or getting worse?

- Do you know how your competitors could seduce your customers?

- Do you know why you've lost certain clients?

These questions are crucial, Zenger says. If you can't collect these data, you're wasting a resource. If nothing else, ask direct questions to get direct answers. Listen to what you learn.

Judge Jeffrey Shuman, who also emphasizes the importance of putting the customer first, evaluates whether a nominated entrepreneur has created a process for continually confirming and anticipating customer needs and desires.

Judge George Dalton says that putting customer relationships first is "so simple, it's hokey!" He has always used annual customer satisfaction surveys, and he swears that he personally reads every CEO-level response. He charges other leaders in his organization to read their peer-level responses as well. If the pile of responses is too high, he says, "I read the ones that express dissatisfaction." Then he calls the customer to confirm that he understands the problem; he does what he and his organization can do to address the problem, and he always calls the customer a second time to be sure that the situation has improved.

Marketing expert Philip Kotler suggests spreading customer focus around. Your company's concentration on value should not be limited to the marketing department. Everyone in your organization should make this commitment. Every department should be customer minded.

For example, research and development should seek customer reactions and suggestions while researching a new product, Kotler says. The manufacturing department should continuously improve product quality and meet customer requirements for customization as much as possible. The sales department should provide feedback on customers' needs and ideas to those who develop products. In short, everyone should think of ways to offer even more customer value.

To help his employees promote and maintain a customer-oriented culture, Michael Dell, for instance, bases his compensation models on the metrics his employees gather about customer experience. As a result, employees track the quality of customer service by event, meaning that every instance of customer contact via every channel is recorded.

As Ernst & Young states in its corporate information online, "We work in an innovative environment that enables us to help our clients anticipate, define, and solve the issues that are important to their success. We have the knowledge, resources, world-class skills, state-of-the-art technology, and creativity to be a trusted business advisor. And we've developed a vast network of strategic alliances to help us deliver solutions even more quickly anywhere in the world." In other words, it's all about the customer.

They say that leaders take people along on the entrepreneurial journey. I think it's the other way around.

—**GEORGE D. DALTON**, *Chairman and CEO of Call Solutions*™

George Dalton recently gave up retirement to start Call Solutions, a full-service customer relationship marketing firm. Before his retirement, Dalton was cofounder and leader of Fiserv, Inc., a financial data processing service organization. He formed Fiserv in 1984 when he merged his company, First Data Processing, with Sunshine State Systems. Under Dalton's leadership, Fiserv grew at a tremendous pace, becoming international, going public, and increasing revenues from $21 million in 1984 to $1.4 billion when he left in 1999.

An active community and business leader, Dalton has received numerous awards and honors, including the Ernst & Young Entrepreneur Of The Year® Award, the Financial World "CEO of the Year Award," and the Harvard Business School Club of Wisconsin and *Milwaukee Journal* Wisconsin Leader of the Year Award. He is a member of the board of directors of Clark/ Bardes, Fiduciary Capital Growth Fund, Inc., FMI Funds, Inc., and Wisconsin Wireless. He also sits on the advisory boards of the Milwaukee Humane Society, Milwaukee Public Museum, Milwaukee School of Engineering, and numerous charitable associations.

COMMUNICATIONS AND MARKETING

Entrepreneurs know that solid internal communications for their workforce and excellent external communications, or marketing, for their customers, are critical in keeping stakeholders informed and creating a cohesive organizational culture.

Communicate simply, fully, and clearly to your internal audience about your company's overall aims or ambitions and how the company is working toward achieving them, author Douglas L. Laurie advises. To be fully engaged and become effective problem solvers, employees need to know more than the everyday tasks expected of them. They also need to understand how their individual job interacts with all of the company's functions.

This approach to internal communications is a pivotal step in building a strong team. Author John H. Zenger suggests that to be a great manager, you've got to have both technical skills and cheerleading skills. To run the company, you've got to keep your people motivated and effective. Do they know where they're going? Do they have a firm grasp of your vision? It's not enough for you to have a vision. You've got to be able to communicate it clearly and quickly—two sentences, max. He advises that you can't change people; they are what they are. But with the right management and the right communications, you can create an environment that encourages people to do and be their best.

Explaining proper external communications—the full panoply of public relations, advertising, and marketing that boosts an entrepreneurial effort—would take a separate book, or many books. The basic concept is that you should emphasize your strengths, put your best assets out for public understanding. If you are at the top of the line technically, if you have the area's most advanced customer service plan, if you are an entrepreneurial star, let your constituency know.

Be aware that marketing is not just selling, although selling is part of marketing, Kotler writes in *Kotler on Marketing*. In fact, when marketing works well, people react positively to what you are offering and sell it to each other by word of mouth.

"Smart marketing companies are improving their customer knowledge, customer connection technologies, and understanding of customer economics. They are inviting customers to codesign the product. They are ready to make flexible marketing offerings," Kotler writes. "Successful companies will be the few that can keep their marketing changing as fast as their marketplace."

Doing market research and creating a marketing plan will help you reach and acquire new customers, according to *The Guru Guide to Entrepreneurship,* because research can tell you the most effective ways to develop, package, price, distribute, and promote your product or service.

As your market shifts, so must your communication message. Your objective is to meet customers' real needs and focus on having a long-term, repeated relationship with satisfied customers.

Entrepreneurs understand that. "Whenever there is a need, there is an opportunity," says Kotler. "Marketing is the art of finding, developing, and profiting from opportunities."

Media relations are a separate concern, and your firm needs a policy on dealing with the media in both easy times and difficult times. *The Guru Guide* suggests that you should contact the press to seek media coverage, which amounts to free publicity. The key is finding an intriguing news angle so you can offer a legitimate news story. Richard Branson, the CEO of Virgin Airways, suggests that you should always be available to the press, plan meetings with them, and treat reporters well. An honest "I'm not able to tell you that now" or "I can't discuss that yet" works better than a furtive "No comment." Telling bad news quickly, briefly, and truthfully is far more effective in the long run than dragging it out, misrepresenting it, or letting it drip out in increasingly dismal increments.

Some forms of educating the marketplace are more subtle than others. Take, for example, Young J. Paik, the 1999 National

Entrepreneur Of The Year in the manufacturing category. Paik overcame several entry barriers when he founded Paco Steel and introduced a new steel I-beam that was lighter and cheaper than the industry standard.

Unfortunately, as Paik recounts, prospective customers weren't interested. "Builders were not convinced of the quality of the new manufacturing technique, and they were reluctant to do business with outsiders, particularly an Asian engineer." Paik was running out of time and money, so he came up with an ingenious idea for promoting his innovation.

He earned his first customer by giving his product away on consignment. The builder liked the Paco I-beam, and word spread about the superiority of Paik's product and services, which have grown to include free engineering services, an on-time delivery guarantee, and extended credit terms. Within ten years, Paco Steel captured a majority share of the steel beam market.

Judges are impressed when winning entrepreneurs use original, creative positioning to gain market entry and recognition. Judge Jim McCann of 1-800-Flowers.com mentions Jack Kahl, a 1991 national finalist for Entrepreneur Of The Year in the manufacturing category. Kahl was the founder and former CEO of Manco Inc., now a Henkel Group company. As McCann tells the story: "Here's a guy who manufactures duct tape, not exactly exciting. It's d-u-c-t tape, like an air duct, but everyone kept calling it duck tape, d-u-c-k. So what does Jack do? He says, 'I'm not going to run away from it. I'm going to go right at it.' So he created a mascot for his company and it was a duck, a big animated duck. So everyone in the company has their duck shirt, the tape has a duck logo, and so on. Jack took a boring manufacturing company and made it fun and exciting by looking for clever new ideas to bring to his company."

Others agree with McCann and the EOY judges who selected Kahl as a regional winner and contender for the national title. Kahl was named one of "America's most admired CEOs" by *IndustryWeek* magazine in 1993. *Inc.* magazine honored him as one of the three CEOs in America who established benchmark leadership practices, and *Cleveland Magazine* named him "the best boss in town" in 1996 and 2000.

David Stassen was the 1998 national Health Care and Life Sciences Entrepreneur Of The Year. He formed Spine-Tech, Inc., so he could market a product—based on the discoveries of Dr. Stephen Kuslich—that revolutionized the treatment of chronic back pain. Before Stassen's spinal implant was available, surgeons used a highly invasive procedure to lessen pressure on degenerated spinal discs. With the advent of the Spine-Tech implant, spinal surgery hospital stays dropped from ten days to one, and the number of patients who reported favorable results rose from the 80th percentile to the mid-90 percentile. Introducing such a novel medical item wasn't easy, says Stassen. "There really wasn't anything like it. There was an awful lot of skepticism from surgeons saying, 'This is a crazy idea.' They had every excuse in the book for why it wouldn't work."

Stassen didn't give up. Instead, he became creative and started a preavailability marketing effort, even though his implant device would not clear the FDA approval process for years. Spine-Tech began an aggressive educational campaign, and by the time the implant was available for sale in late 1996, Stassen had created pent-up customer demand. First-year sales surpassed his initial target and reached $58 million. In time, sales jumped to hundreds of millions of dollars, and Stassen sold his company to Sulza Medica, a Swedish orthopedics company. By then, Spine-Tech researchers had already begun looking for ways to stimulate new bone growth. David Stassen and his leadership team never had a problem thinking big or using marketing to their advantage.

COMMUNITY SERVICE

Entrepreneur Of The Year judges pay special attention to the way entrepreneurs and their companies give back to their communities. As Harris and Brannick advise, internally aligned companies know they need to create an image as community leaders. These companies cultivate a strong reputation in relevant industries and support local, regional, and national initiatives for social causes.

Ernst & Young, for example, has a long-standing tradition of philanthropy through its support of institutions of higher education, civic and cultural agencies, and the communities in which the firm operates. The company sponsors grants, symposia, professorships, and other activities at colleges and universities; promotes issues of importance to its profession; and enthusiastically supports the arts. Ernst & Young and its international workforce contributed more than $4 million toward relief efforts following the September 11, 2001, terrorist attacks on the World Trade Center in New York City.

Almost all Entrepreneur Of The Year winners carry out community service programs and offer philanthropic funding. Just among the 2001 national winners in the United States, for example, judges praised these philanthropic efforts:

- *Master Entrepreneur Of The Year: Samuel C. Johnson,* of S.C. Johnson & Son, Inc., retired recently but continues his dedication to environmental and conservation efforts.

- *Robert N. Thompson, the Real Estate Entrepreneur Of The Year,* heads R.N. Thompson & Associates, Inc., which began with $12 and a rented tractor and became a multi-million-dollar real estate development firm. His success allows him to share with others, demonstrating what he calls "the abundance mentality." Thompson asserts, "There's plenty in the world. Sharing the abundance is just the natural thing to do." For Thompson, that means supporting community institutions, including the St. Mary's Child Center in Indianapolis.

- *Catherine Muller, the Entrepreneur Of The Year Supporter of Entrepreneurship,* retired from Cisco at 46. She wanted to blend her business and technology experience with her passion for social change. Her solution was to launch the Three Guineas Fund, a hybrid foundation that combines program development with grant making. The fund's name is taken from the title of a Virginia Woolf essay in which a person is asked to donate one guinea to a cause to prevent war, one to educate women, and one to promote employment. The Three Guineas Fund's largest project, the Women's Technology Cluster (WTC), is the first business incubator for tech start-ups with women principals. It also encourages philanthropy in young businesses by requiring 2 percent of equity to be reinvested in WTC programs and the community.

- *Jon M. and Karen Huntsman of the Huntsman Cancer Institute* in Salt Lake City, Utah, received the 2001 Entrepreneur Of The Year Award for Principle-Centered Leadership presented by the Franklin Covey Company. Jon Huntsman's life and career are proof that one person can make a difference. Huntsman has used his considerable business success—first with Huntsman Container Cor- poration, then with the multinational Huntsman Corporation, the world's largest privately held chemical company—as a way to give something back. His goal is not to build profits but to use them to enrich the human soul and alleviate suffering. Huntsman, a cancer survivor himself, and his wife, Karen, are committed to eradicating the disease and have funded a number of state-of-the-art cancer treatment and research facilities. Huntsman donates such a large portion of his profits to humanitarian projects worldwide that the *Journal of Philanthropy* named him the United States' third most generous philanthropist.

These benchmark entrepreneurial leaders demonstrate the weight that the Entrepreneur Of The Year competition places on community service. By professional standards, giving back to the community is the right thing to do—and, by the way, it's very good for business.

ETHICAL VALUES AND ATTITUDES

Leaders face ethical dilemmas at every level. The best leaders do what is right, not just what's quick or easy. It often takes great courage to do the right thing, even when the right action is obvious. For good or ill, leaders set a moral and ethical example for their followers, according to *Leadership: Enhancing the Lessons of Experience,* by Richard L. Hughes, Robert C. Ginnett, and Gordon J. Curphy. Many studies attempt to define values, ethics, and morals; determine how values develop; how values are passed on to others; and how values can change and can affect leadership.

Many actions are legal, yet unethical, say the authors, including scapegoating, shirking responsibility, knowingly making unreasonable demands, breaking promises, and giving desirable assignments to friends, even though other people are more qualified.

BEN & JERRY'S HOMEMADE, INC.

Entrepreneur Of The Year winners Ben and Jerry's have always been proactive about philanthropy. Ben & Jerry's Homemade, Inc., the Vermont-based manufacturer of ice cream, frozen yogurt, and sorbet, was founded in 1978 in a renovated gas station in Burlington, Vermont, by childhood friends Ben Cohen and Jerry Greenfield with a $12,000 investment ($4,000 of which was borrowed from Ben's father). The ice cream, made from fresh Vermont milk and cream, soon became popular for its innovative flavors. According to its Web site, the company currently distributes ice cream, low-fat ice cream, frozen yogurt, sorbet, and novelty products nationwide as well as in selected foreign countries in supermarkets, grocery stores, convenience stores, franchised Ben & Jerry's scoop shops, restaurants, and other venues.

In 1988, Ben & Jerry's Homemade, Inc., issued a mission statement declaring that the firm is dedicated to the creation and demonstration of a new corporate concept of linked prosperity. It establishes a mission of three interrelated parts: product, economic, and social. "Underlying the mission," the statement reads, "is the determination to seek new and creative ways of addressing product, economic and social concerns, while holding a deep respect for individuals inside and outside the company, and for the communities of which they are a part."

The firm's product mission covers making, distributing, and selling the finest quality all-natural ice cream and related products in a wide variety of innovative flavors made from Vermont dairy products. The economic plank of its platform calls for operating the company on a sound financial basis of profitable growth, increasing value for shareholders, and creating career opportunities and financial rewards for employees.

But it is the social platform that has created Ben & Jerry's reputation for outstanding community service. It states that the firm intends to operate "in a way that actively recognizes the central role that business plays in the structure of society by initiating innovative ways to improve the quality of life of a broad community—local, national, and international."

According to author Ann Svendson, the leadership team uses their stated mission and goals as the basis for auditing the firm's social performance. The company codified social goals for its staff, shareholders, customers, franchisees, and those who receive its corporate philanthropy.

The company's Web site informs grant seekers that it gives away approximately 7.5 percent of its pretax earnings in three ways:

1. Employee community action teams at five Vermont sites, which distribute small grants to community groups in the state

2. Corporate grants made by the company's Director of Social Mission Development

3. The Ben & Jerry's Foundation, which is managed by a nine-member employee board and considers proposals relating to children and families, disadvantaged groups, and the environment

Overall, Ben & Jerry's supports "projects which are models for social change—projects which exhibit creative problem solving and hopefulness."

Ben & Jerry's Foundation was established in 1985 through a donation of stock in Ben & Jerry's Homemade, Inc., funds that are used as an endowment. In addition, Ben & Jerry's makes donations at its board's discretion from its pretax profits. The foundation receives a portion of these funds, and an additional portion is earmarked for the employee-led Community Action Teams.

The foundation's stated mission is "to make the world a better place by empowering Ben & Jerry's employees to use available resources to support and encourage organizations that are working toward eliminating the underlying causes of environmental and social problems."

The foundation offers "competitive grants to not-for-profit, grassroots organizations throughout the United States which facilitate progressive social change by addressing the underlying conditions of societal and environmental problems," according to the firm's Web site. It focuses on the types of activities and strategies an organization uses for creating social change. The foundation considers only proposals from "grassroots, constituent-led organizations that are organizing for systemic social change." And it supports "programs and projects that are examples of creative problem solving."

Studies cited in the book show that leaders' attitudes about themselves may not coincide with how followers see them, and leaders' attitudes about followers don't always coincide with how followers see themselves. Stereotyping according to gender, race, religion, age, culture, or other criteria has an impact on leadership and thus creates advancement obstacles for women, minorities, the young, and the old much greater to overcome than those faced by others.

How leaders address problem solving, team building, delegating, and many other aspects of their job are highly influenced by their own ethics and values. Some organizations sacrifice character in the name of profit, but the lack of character always comes back to haunt them in some way, the authors warn, whether in low employee morale, bad public relations, organizational chaos, or other undesirable effects.

Business writer John Zenger offers two suggestions for productivity that show the power of ethical behavior in action.

The first: listen to the truth and tell the truth. To do this, you have to *know the truth*. Are your people afraid to tell you about mistakes? Do they sugarcoat the truth so you only hear part of it? If you want the truth, you must never get irritated when someone reports bad news to you. Then it's your job to tell people what to do with the truth. Share serious news with your group and explain honestly how it affects their life—salaries, benefits, and continued employment. Because employees are likely to forget your pronouncements, repeat the important things. Then repeat them again.

The second suggestion: take responsibility. An entrepreneur and as a leader, you must take responsibility for the performance of your outfit—no matter what. If you delegate a project to someone who screws up, you're part of the screwup. Either you didn't support the project sufficiently or you delegated it to the wrong person. Take credit when something works, but don't take it all. Acknowledge employees' efforts.

The day will come in your business when the line between ethical and nonethical behavior may seem unclear, but it's a deep divide. If you aren't sure, ask someone whose principles you admire. And if you are going to err, err on the side of being particularly ethical. This is not a matter where fudging works. By holding yourself to the highest principles and ethical standards, you can hold your leadership team and your employees to the same nonnegotiable standards. You can look to the Entrepreneur Of The Year Award Program for numerous stellar examples of principled leadership, an attitude that has always been made the highest priority in the judging process.

All Entrepreneur Of The Year winners are eligible for the National Entrepreneur Of The Year Award for Principle-Centered Leadership. This award, presented by the Franklin Covey Company, goes to a person whose leadership style has demonstrated ethics and integrity and who has shown a proven commitment to empowering the people under them and contributing to the community. The 2000 winner was Jack Lowe, Jr., CEO of TD Industries, a multi-million-dollar construction company that is 75 percent employee owned.

Lowe's secret is that he believes in "servant leadership," the concept that leaders exist to serve those who work for them. Lowe contends that even though some may question this management style, he has learned that it works. In fact, his experience is that "it works better." Want proof? Since 1997, TD Industries' revenues increased by 30 percent from 1999 to 2000, and *Fortune* magazine listed the company as one of the top ten places to work. Lowe says that by creating a great place to work and by having outstanding customer service, his business makes "good money." That's what happens with principled leadership: success is "a natural consequence of getting the other stuff right."

The Entrepreneur Of The Year Award for Principle-Centered Leadership recognizes entrepreneurs who have achieved outstanding business success in a principled manner. The entrepreneurs who win this particular honor have a sense of ethics, mission, integrity, and stewardship about their life and work. They respect and empower other people, from their management team to their employees, customers, and colleagues. This, in turn, fosters a sense of trust among those stakeholders and the community at large. And when you are building a team, that is exactly what you want.

CHAPTER 4

Innovation

BREAKING THE MOLD

"Whatever you can do, or dream you can, begin it. Boldness has genius, power, and magic in it."

—**M.H. LAWRENCE**, *The Scottish Himalayan Expedition*

An organization needs two types of people: those who come up with ideas and those who execute ideas, says judge William Saito. An entrepreneur is both. After all, the existence of a successful company run by its founder proves that an entrepreneur can start with an idea and build a business around it. But that doesn't mean it's easy.

You can learn a lot by watching entrepreneurs test new waters, push boundaries, beat the odds, and triumph in the face of adversity. When entrepreneurs launch a new business or manage it through turbulent times, Entrepreneur Of The Year judges examine how they applied innovation and perseverance to conquer their challenges.

Entrepreneurs need invention and creativity to ensure successful development along with the marketing and distribution of new products and services. They also need personal stamina, ample knowledge, sufficient investment, and strong financial management, but that's the topic of the next chapter. For now, as judge Shuman says, all businesses have to pay attention to three core processes: how you get and keep your customers; how you develop innovative products; and how you fulfill your service. To accomplish these steps, "it is critically important to have innovative processes in place."

Judges define innovation as invention, originality, and creativity as evidenced by new or improved technologies, products, services, and/or approaches to business. They also see it evidenced in corporate cultures that develop a sense of urgency about continuous improvement and change.

In business, nothing stands still for very long. So as economies, politics, industries, and technology shift, entrepreneurs must be able to follow the roller coaster. At critical times—or before a crisis hits if they are very savvy businesspeople—entrepreneurs invent and reinvent when they must, and they solve problems creatively.

These seismic shifts come in at least three guises:

1. *Innovation.* Changes you initiate and decide to make yourself from creativity, prescience, or pure invention.

2. *Adaptation.* Changes you make to manage the impact of new circumstances in your company, industry, or marketplace.

3. *Challenges.* Changes you make when you must overcome barriers, defeat difficult circumstances, or rescue your business.

Entrepreneurs must deal with change in all these guises as well as change that comes dressed in other, even more unpredictable, costumes. Fortunately, entrepreneurs—hardy souls who are driven to begin their own companies in the first place—

are already more inventive and adaptable than most folks just by their nature.

Ernst & Young Entrepreneur Of The Year Award judges have seen entrepreneurs who founded their business based on amazingly original products or business models. They have seen entrepreneurs who shifted direction on a dime to keep their company growing. And they have seen businesspeople who survived times of daunting adversity by repositioning and reinventing themselves and their company.

That sets the path for this chapter: Following the judges as they observe entrepreneurs enduring the process of creativity and originality, facing and dealing with adaptation to change, and winning the battle in overcoming adversity.

INNOVATION AND CREATIVITY

"Innovation requires that you ask yourself, 'How can I get to the same place but differently? What can I do to add value to an already known process?"

—JUDGE ROBERT VUKOVICH

To distinguish an Entrepreneur Of The Year from other accomplished entrepreneurs, judges assess candidates on many factors, including innovation and creativity. The judges ask the following questions as criteria to analyze a nominee's ability to innovate:

- Has the candidate pioneered a new approach or technology?

- Has the candidate anticipated or embraced change in the competitive environment in an innovative way?

- Has the candidate created a corporate culture of innovation?

The leaders of a company with an innovation-driven culture are characterized by their passion to "create and shape the future"—and to do so better and more quickly than the competition, say authors Jim Harris and Jean Brannick in *Finding and Keeping Great Employees.* Innovation-driven organizations develop new products and services as quickly as they can, constantly cannibalizing their latest and greatest to create something newer and better. These companies cultivate a sense of adventure and push the limits, giving employees the freedom to take their intelligence and creativity as far as they can.

This unbounded culture has an underlying purpose: to establish an environment that unleashes people's limitless creativity, enthusiasm, and energy, and thus to create and shape the company's future.

Judge William Saito advises that to build an innovative culture, you should hire creative people. He uses a set of brainteasers—devices that are well known in technical recruiting circles—to compel candidates to invent answers that help reveal how they think through a problem to arrive at a solution. For example, he might ask an interview candidate, "Why are manhole covers round?" He might also present the following puzzle: You have a single gold bar. You have to make two cuts of the gold bar and pay someone equal amounts for seven days. How do you pay the person? Judge Saito explains that "the questions are actually very basic computer optimization-type questions that show the creativity and innovation in a person's style."

Once they have hired creative people, entrepreneurs rely on employee contributions to spark innovation in all facets of their business, from employee relations and human resources policies to ad hoc customer relationship management.

To get people to work on a particular vision and focus their energy and create . . . that's not science, it's art . . . the interpretation of a vision.

—**WILLIAM H. SAITO**, *Cofounder, President, CEO, and Chairman of I/O Software*

In addition to his role as a judge, William Saito has contributed considerably to the Entrepreneur Of The Year Awards. In 2000, he participated in Japan's entry into the Ernst & Young Entrepreneur Of The Year Award.

Saito cofounded I/O Software to translate, localize, and port American software applications for sale in Japan. Since 1991, the company has evolved into a major security software provider with a wide range of applications that support user authentication technologies, including biometrics, Public Key Infrastructure (PKI), and smart cards.

I/O Software products include commercial applications that range from enterprise-level network security, electronic commerce, and encryption to information access on PCs and PDAs. I/O Software is the only company whose biometric user-authentication technology will be integrated into the next generation of Microsoft's Windows operating system. In addition, I/O Software has established close relationships with a growing number of major companies within the industry, including an agreement with Intel to use I/O Software technology for preboot authentication.

William Saito is active in industry, civic, and charitable organizations and serves on a number of boards for the University of California Riverside.

Like detectives on the trail of a big case, Entrepreneur Of The Year judges search diligently for companies with genuinely creative cultures.

Judge Jim McCann asks nominees:

- What have you done differently?

- How is it clever?

- How did you take an idea from one arena and play with it in another?

- What's the sparkle that makes your company interesting, creative, and fun for the staff, the community, and the customer?

Judge Steve Papermaster has a parallel list of questions:

- How original was the way you started the business and then expanded it?

- Do you use innovation and creativity to overcome obstacles?

- Have you fostered a culture that encourages innovation and acts on it?

Judges who are assessing innovation want to know if a company has "done something that dramatically changes how people behave or how we think about things or how business takes place," says facilitator Ray Smilor. "Has the company . . . catapulted something new into the marketplace?" By this he means a major innovation, such as the creation of E*Trade, which "fundamentally changed how people interact with the stock market."

E*TRADE

E*Trade's founder, William Porter, and its current chairman and CEO, Christos M. Cotsakos, were the National Entrepreneurs Of The Year in the Internet products and services category in 1998. If EOY gave an award for innovation, they would have been top contenders.

In an effort to capitalize on the public's emerging ability to access stock quotes through the Internet, Porter—a physicist and inventor with more than a dozen patents—founded E*Trade as a service bureau in 1982. The first customer was a doctor in Michigan, who placed the initial online transaction using E*Trade securities technology on July 11, 1983.

What began with a single click nearly 20 years ago is now a daily part of life for E*Trade Financial households worldwide, according to the firm's Web site. By 1992, Porter launched one of the original all-electronic brokerages and began offering online investing services through America Online and CompuServe. In essence, E*Trade took the middleman out of personal stock market investing and put portfolio management firmly in the hands of customers.

In 1996, Porter handed over the reins to Christos M. Cotsakos, a decorated Vietnam War veteran who earned a Purple Heart and Bronze Star for valor. Christos came to E*Trade Group with more than 20 years of senior management experience at Federal Express and A.C. Neilsen, where he served as president, co-CEO and director.

That year, under Cotsakos's direction, the E*Trade Group, Inc., launched <www.etrade.com>, which led to an explosion in public demand for the company's services. For the first time, individual investors could use the Internet for automated, personalized access to brokerage services, 24 hours a day, 7 days a week.

With that, the company shifted into high gear. From its humble beginnings as a discount brokerage, E*Trade reinvented itself and grew into a global leader in personal financial services with branded Web sites in several countries.

E*Trade Financial brings together personalized and integrated products and services to meet individual customers' complex investing, banking, lending, and planning needs. E*Trade Financial brings together expanded access to financial services and personal one-on-one assistance from licensed Financial Services Associates via a variety of touch points, including any of five E*Trade Financial Centers in New York, Boston, Denver, Beverly Hills, and San Francisco, and through various E*Trade Financial Zones across the United States.

Customers can also access their accounts via a network of more than 11,000 E*Trade Financial ATMs and kiosks. Through personalized Digital Financial Media initiatives, the company continues to be a leader in providing "anytime, anywhere, any device" access to financial information and transaction capabilities, delivering branded, original E*Trade Financial content each day from its broadcast studios in New York and San Francisco.

Today, the E*Trade Group's leadership team, based at corporate headquarters in Menlo Park, California, is comprised of seasoned industry veterans from technology, operations, finance, and marketing. Because of its reputation for innovation, the company is able to recruit and select employees from an international pool of talent.

E*Trade went public in August 1996 and completed a follow-on offering one year later. The company's common stock trades on the New York Stock Exchange under the symbol ET. Its options trade on the Chicago Board Options Exchange and the American Stock Exchange under the option root symbol ET.

E*Trade's focus remains clear: to use technology to set the standard for innovation, service, and value for households seeking more control over their finances.

Judge Steve Papermaster sees a lot of truth in the notion "that there is no such thing as an original thought, that history is repeated over and over again," so when he measures innovation, he's not necessarily looking for a totally new idea as much as he is assessing "the strength of execution. How original was the way the entrepreneur tried to start the business or grow it?" In contrast, judge Victoria Jackson measures innovation in two parts: the concept and the individual effort.

As the criteria reveal, the judges look for innovative concepts in products and services, and in the company's business model or positioning in the industry. Why? Well, among other reasons, because it is easier to measure business performance than it is to assess an entrepreneur's personal creativity or originality. Yet in an effort to take that measurement, judges ask two basic, albeit different, questions:

1. Is the entrepreneur inventive and open to opportunities that stem from changes in technology, society, and the relevant industry?

2. What has the entrepreneur done to foster and implement innovation throughout a company? Or an industry?

An effective innovator can change the way an entire industry functions, as demonstrated by Stuart Weitzman, the famous shoe designer and manufacturer and a 1999 Master Entrepreneur Of The Year national finalist. Weitzman creates expensive, high-fashion footwear with unique materials, such as the part-platinum stilettos bedecked with diamonds that an actress wore to the 2002 Annual Academy Awards.

Weitzman's innovative management style—which fostered the careers of those around him as they provided the support systems he needed—brought him to the attention of EOY judges. "I didn't have places to go for capital," Weitzman says, "so I found some entrepreneurial executives and encouraged them to set up their own periphery businesses." Today, his employees manage two retail stores and run firms that handle advertising and public relations, marketing and retail consulting, and services and showroom management—and all of their companies work exclusively for Stuart Weitzman, Inc.

These entrepreneurs' stories embody the intelligent application of innovation, which—like other resources—must be harnessed productively. That is the magic ingredient that turns innovation into solid businesses.

"Entrepreneurs are people who see what others don't see," judge Robert Vukovich says, "and they have the gift of looking at something and seeing it differently. Instead of seeing a glass of water, they see fluid dynamics. While other people might look at a spring, entrepreneurs see an article that has potential energy."

But if you are going to see what others miss, your vision has to be strong and you have to filter a lot of information.

That is why Vukovich "reads prodigiously," and it pays off for him; as he says, he gets a lot of ideas for his health sciences work from reading. "I get into the nitty-gritty of what's going on in medicine, and I keep my finger on the pulse of the industry and the general economy. I follow what competitive companies are doing by monitoring their press releases. I make sure I don't miss too much in terms of technology that could result in new therapeutics."

To provoke his creative thinking and to measure the way entrepreneurs think creatively, he asks:

- How can something be done differently?

- What can be done to add value to a process?

When entrepreneurs look for ways to add value to or improve something, they are usually solving a problem. At his company, judge William Saito makes problem solving a group process. "I like to throw out ideas and then try to get everyone involved creatively. I like to debate and become the devil's advocate. That's how great ideas come about."

When other judges describe the creative process, Saito's debates or brainstorms are a perfect fit. Like other judges who advocate paying attention to world events to find new ideas, Saito advocates conducting multiple conversations to garner diverse points of view: "Talking to people and bouncing ideas off them is extremely important. Otherwise, we don't come up with anything new." He adds that in his firm debate produces lots of small "eurekas." "Not a eureka like inventing the wheel. Innovations don't happen all of a sudden. They build up, and something is created that is unique, different, and defensible."

For example, in 1957 Jack Taylor had an innovative idea: people might like to rent cars for a few days at a time, perhaps while their own car was being repaired. A lot of people told him it would never work, but Taylor's innovative insight became Enterprise Rent-A-Car, which now has 500,000 vehicles. Today, Jack Taylor's brainstorm is the largest car rental company in North America.

Like Jack Taylor, innovative entrepreneurs can actually create new markets.

J. Renee Claxton did it.

Claxton, a 1998 regional Entrepreneur Of The Year, spent many years in the retail garment industry. She realized over time that clothing retailers needed a service that didn't—yet—exist, a support business to inspect clothing and provide quality control. She defied the naysayers, who weren't convinced of the opportunity Claxton spied, and she created a one-of-a-kind company called Sort & Pack.

ENTERPRISE RENT-A-CAR

Enterprise Rent-A-Car's founder Jack Taylor, the 1997 Entrepreneur Of The Year, began his company under the name Executive Leasing in 1957 in a cramped office in the basement of his St. Louis Cadillac dealership. Because the office was next to the body shop, leasing salesmen had to scream into the phone to be heard over the rattle of body shop machines.

Though auto leasing was not a common practice at the time, Taylor had a gut instinct that consumers would see the benefits of leasing automobiles rather than buying them. His critics, however, thought leasing would never work. The concept was too new, too innovative. Yet according to the firm's Web site, by maintaining steadfast commitment to personal service and demonstrating the advantages of leasing, Enterprise's first venture took root.

Given this focus on exceptional customer service and convenience, Enterprise has become the largest car rental company in North America and is a leader in the field of fleet services. The Web site's timeline, from 1957 to 1999, shows steady growth, an expanding fleet of cars, and an expanding geographic scope. The firm, which now has 50,000 employees, is active in cities across the United States and in the United Kingdom, Canada, and Germany. By 1999 the company had 4,000 locations worldwide and a fleet of 500,000 vehicles. Its Andrew1-800-Rent-A-Car line receives reservations around the clock.

From the beginning, Jack Taylor wanted to hire people who would be not merely employees but entrepreneurs themselves. Looking for loyal employees willing to learn how to do business and to try something new, Jack hired and trained staff members who may have been unqualified but were undeniably eager. After they were trained, he let them loose. According to Enterprise's retired vice president, Wayne Kaufman, "Jack is a person who delegates authority and allows you to do the job yourself."

Instead of giving employees flat salaries, Taylor instituted an aggressive profit-sharing plan and incentive rewards program that placed no limits on the amount of bonus pay an employee could earn. Everyone at the company is rewarded financially for a job well done, from counter agents to branch managers. In fact, top sales managers at Enterprise can earn incomes near that of the CEO's.

In terms of hiring, Enterprise is the largest college recruiter in the country and received *Fortune* magazine's recognition as one of the "100 Best Companies to Work For." The company's statement about this accolade notes that Enterprise was included on the list because it hires management trainees and "moves them quickly into management positions, in which they share in their local branches' profits. Enterprise throws a lot of parties to keep it fun."

Jack Taylor's son, Andy, is now the chairman and CEO of the company, which still focuses more on renting to the local community than on renting to tourists. Enterprise serves customers who are having their car repaired, who need a different car for a special occasion, or who are taking a short business or leisure trip. Enterprise also manages fleets for other firms, sells preowned cars, and, in a creative program it developed, supplies "Rideshare" vans to groups of coworkers who wish to commute.

The company is famous for its advertising slogan, "Pick Enterprise. We'll pick you up," and for the innovative pick-up service cited in its ads. When you want to rent an Enterprise vehicle, you phone them and they'll come to get you. After all, if you had an available car, you wouldn't need them.

In a Web site interview, Andy Taylor explains: "We've worked to create an environment rich with growth and opportunity. We promote from within based on performance and merit, not seniority. Our culture allows employees to take ownership of their career. They make it happen.

"The unique culture that my father, Jack Taylor, developed helped get us where we are today. It is a culture where we trust our employees at the local level to make the right decisions, and they trust us to provide the support needed—and no more—from our corporate headquarters. It's a balance that is hard to replicate and is what has allowed our people to drive the growth themselves.

"Others have studied our organization and tried to change what they already had to something less centralized. It's been a lot easier for us, I'd guess, because that's the way it has always been," Taylor adds.

"Each of the offices operates as a small business, giving employees the autonomy and authority to meet the local needs of customers. Branch managers have control of marketing initiatives, staff, customer service, and accounts receivables. Also, branch managers work directly with their own profit and loss statements to determine their success and failure opportunities."

In a separate interview on the Enterprise Web site, Taylor adds that Enterprise is "also a friendly place to work, made up of energetic, outgoing people. Basically, employees have a lot of fun working at Enterprise."

He should know; he started as a vacation employee. "My first job with Enterprise was when I was 16 years old," Taylor says. "During Christmas and summer vacations I would help move cars from one location to another and would help out customers at the front counter."

"A high-loyalty company has a clear conception of how to provide superior value to a target set of customers," writes Frederick F. Reichheld, author of *The Loyalty Effect*. "Take, for example, Enterprise Rent-A-Car. It was initially in the insurance market. If you had a car accident, it would provide a replacement car. And the discipline not to grow willy-nilly into other areas, like the airport-vacation market, allowed it to tune up a business system that was really superior for its target customers.

"Enterprise saw that more and more customers needed something extra, like a large car to take the kids to college or a third car when the mother-in-law visits from Florida for a month. So instead of winning a new base of customers, the company stuck with its original customers and extended the value proposition with them, which I think is brilliant.

"And then what does it do?" Reichheld asks. "Enterprise sets itself up as a series of local businesses and shares the profits with the local partner. When you do that, you can attract terrific talent that stays with you and delivers amazing performance. Enterprise has great partnerships, the talent is awesome, and it's built so much internal cash generation that it has more than 300,000 cars in its fleet and has never had to go outside to raise capital."

Enterprise is also active in serving its community under the aegis of the Enterprise Foundation headed by Andy's sister, Jo Ann Taylor Kindle. In 2001 the Foundation donated $25 million to Washington University in St. Louis to endow a permanent fund for scholarships for 30 to 40 African American and financially disadvantaged students each year.

Andy Taylor said that the company and the family made the gift to support a "world-class university located in Enterprise's hometown." The corporate statement notes that the Taylor family strongly believes the strength and overall excellent reputation of the local university also serves as a magnet to attract talented individuals to the region. Jack and Andy Taylor both serve on the university's board of trustees.

Andy Taylor sums up the company's approach: "Today, Enterprise's business philosophy is the same as my father's was when he started the business 42 years ago. Enterprise strives to offer customers great service while developing and training our employees for future opportunities."

In fact, a J.D. Power and Associates study ranked Enterprise first in customer satisfaction among leisure rentals at or near airports. The firm serves 97 of the top 100 airports in the continental United States and provides airport rates that are up to 20 percent lower than its competitors.

"Our goal at Enterprise never has been to be the biggest, but the best, so we're thrilled with the results of this study," Taylor said. "We want to be the airport rental car provider that travelers seek because they prefer our favorable prices and personalized brand of service, from helping with luggage to giving directions to showing customers where to find the windshield wiper switch.

"We believe the study illustrates our loyalty to customers. Enterprise employees' personal service shows our customers just how much we value them—all of them. We provide superior customer service to all air travelers, not just a select group of frequent flyers. That's what keeps them coming back not only to our airport facilities but our nonairport locations as well.

"I don't know what works for other companies," he says, "but my advice to other entrepreneurs is to make sure you treat your customers well, train your employees and offer them future opportunities, and worry about the bottom line last. If you are taking care of the first two, the bottom line will follow. That's our philosophy."

Unable to get a business loan from her bank, Claxton used her savings and the proceeds of a home equity loan to finance her start-up. In other words, she bet her house on her instinct that a brand new business, an idea no one had ever pursued before, would work.

At first, she relied on friends and family members who volunteered to share her workload, which soared quickly. Within three years, Claxton had to move her staff of 25 into a 10,000-square-foot distribution center. She opened a retail outlet on the Ohio State University campus to sell the flawed clothing that her customers rejected. Today, Sort & Pack, Inc., earns more than $2 million a year.

Facilitator Ray Smilor says that Robert D. Basham, Chris Sullivan, and Tim Gannon, the 1994 National Ernst & Young Entrepreneurs Of The Year, provide another great example of how entrepreneurs who can find the right niche don't need to create "the next big thing" to be successful innovators.

The trio found a perfect niche when they created Outback Steakhouse restaurants. The founders made their restaurant chain unique by adding an Australian theme to upscale but casual steakhouse dining.

First, Basham and Sullivan picked up on the growing American interest in the lore of Australian culture. In 1987, when the restaurateurs were still working out the details of their business, *Crocodile Dundee II* was in movie theaters and the movie's star, Paul Hogan, was also appearing in Subaru Outback automobile commercials set in the Australian wilds.

In addition to their catchy marketing theme and some operational innovations, such as serving only dinner, the Outback Steakhouse founders also established an unprecedented management compensation practice. Restaurant managers who signed a five-year contract and invested $25,000 when they were hired became "proprietors" of the restaurant they managed. Managers handled day-to-day operations in return for a standard base pay plus 10 percent of the yearly cash flow from their location. For many of Outback managers, that amounted to an annual salary of more than $100,000. Managers also receive 4,000 shares of stock options that vest over their five-year contract period.

The Outback founders explain that sharing ownership and wealth with location managers benefits the business and its customers several ways:

- It minimizes management turnover, giving managers and employees more time to work together as a team and perfect their jobs.

- It enables the restaurant managers to establish roots in the community, often leading to sponsorship of charitable events and promotions tied to local happenings.

- It attracts veteran managers, whose experience signifies a commitment to their career and an ability to perform.

"We wanted good managers who would think like owners," explains Basham. He added that by investing an amount that, in many cases, amounted to their entire life savings, managers would "have that entrepreneurial flame burning inside them."

The Outback's policy of giving their managers generous, performance-based rewards didn't stop after five years. Interested managers could sign on as joint venture partners (JVPs) for franchise groups or they could "cash out" from their restaurant, taking 10 percent of the average cash flow from the last two years of work multiplied by five. The latter plan provides a long-term incentive for managers to make their location successful.

Outback's creative compensation, operational, and marketing strategies work. It is one of the fastest growing restaurant chains in the United States, with total company revenues of $2.1 billion in 2001 and an almost 17 percent increase in earnings over the past five years. Outback's success is not a surprise, as it has consistently received high customer satisfaction ratings in *Restaurants & Institutions* magazine's annual "Choice In Chains" survey. In addition, Outback, which now has locations in 21 countries, has expanded to include such brands as Carraba's, Fleming's Prime Steakhouse and Wine Bar, and Lee Roy Selmon's.

The Outback demonstrates that an innovative, unconventional approach to finding the right business niche can be a winning strategy. "This has worked only because we dared to do it a lot differently," says Sullivan.

Judge William Mays comments that many entrepreneurs gain their foothold, as Sort & Pack and The Outback Steakhouse did, by innovatively identifying or creating a niche market opportunity within an existing industry: "I think the successful entrepreneur has the uncanny ability to find a niche, something that is always there and that seems like plain common sense, but that nobody else has tried."

You have to be careful when you want to try something innovative, according to some examples of entrepreneurs who ignored discouraging words. Just look at these staggering failures to understand entrepreneurial thinking as reported by James M. Kouzes and Barry Z. Posner in *The Future of Leadership*:

- In 1899, the U.S. Commissioner of Patents, one Charles Duell, declared, "Everything that can be invented has been invented."

- In 1962, Decca Records declared that "guitar music is on the way out" and turned down a group called the Beatles.

- Fred Smith once wrote a student paper proposing an overnight delivery service. His professor noted: "The concept is interesting and well-formed, but in order to earn better than a 'C,' the idea must be feasible." Today, Smith's idea is Federal Express.

- Even the all-time king of the entrepreneurs, Bill Gates, once insisted that "640K of memory ought to be enough for anybody."

Many Entrepreneur Of The Year judges develop their own talent-spotting antenna as they reward entrepreneurs who carve out a new market segment, transform an existing industry, or invent a new business.

Michael Dell's business model—selling computers on a build-to-order, low inventory, direct-from-the-manufacturer, catalog basis—is one of the most famous examples of an entrepreneur who pierced a market already ruled by well-established brands when he provided a lower-cost alternative that gives the consumer better or equal value.

Another example is eBay's Pierre Omidyar, the 1999 National Entrepreneur Of The Year in the Internet category. Omidyar was the first entrepreneur to find a way to make a profitable business from auctions and Web-based trading. He combined the well-established models of community swap meets and auction-style bidding on the Web, creating a method to let people sell anything and buy anything any time, no matter where they are.

Omidyar used *bisociation,* bringing two disparate things together to make a cohesive whole. Judges often use this term to describe the workings of the creative mind. Arthur Koestler coined the term *bisociation*—the result of a creative thinker connecting two unrelated concepts to create a new one—in his book *The Art of Creation.*

Facilitator Ray Smilor believes that some notable Entrepreneur Of The Year winners were able to create their company because of their ability to bisociate; for example:

- Jim McCann, who matched flowers with a phone number to build 1-800-Flowers.com

- Pleasant T. Rowland, who mixed doll making with American history to form the Pleasant Company

- Michael Dell, who combined computers and mail order to launch Dell Computer Corporation

Judges also reward entrepreneurs who find their innovation—their creative sparks—in very disparate places. For example, judge George Dalton says that he doesn't create anything that is completely original, but he "repackages" ideas, products, services, and processes from places other than their origin.

Judge McCann echoes Dalton. "I'm pretty good at adapting," he admits. "I consume periodicals, and my antenna is up all the time. When I see good ideas used in one place, I always ask, 'What can we do in our world that would be similar?' For example, if I see a great idea in manufacturing, I take it, twist it, and introduce it into our retail environment. So ideas don't have to be original, but they become innovative when they are adapted from one arena into another."

This ability to retrofit ideas flexibly and apply new ways of getting things done translates into another important area and one that is more difficult of achievement than pure creativity: adapting to change.

ADAPTATION AND FLEXIBILITY

"There are two kinds of companies: those who change and those who disappear."

—**PHILIP KOTLER,** Kotler on Marketing

"Some of the things people have to ask themselves to know if they are entrepreneurs are, What is my tolerance for ambiguity? How comfortable am I with not knowing what a situation is going to look like a month from now? How comfortable am I with knowing that even though I have a plan, something could happen and I'll have to do something completely different?"

—**JIM MCCANN**

If you think the experts, the judges, and the entrepreneurs have a lot to say about change, you're right. When the unexpected happens, it can come from any direction, and only those who are adaptable and light on their feet will remain standing.

The judges look for entrepreneurs who can effectively counter the negative effects of change, but they shake their heads over the ones who can't. High points go to entrepreneurs who inject new growth into their company when sales, revenues, or the number of new customers levels off or declines. The judges also have lauded entrepreneurs who overcome mistakes and misjudgments or returned from the brink of disaster. Of course, Entrepreneur Of The Year judges don't expect entrepreneurs to have perfect records. Most people get along in business, as in life, by making mistakes and learning from them.

> *"Do leaders need to act confidently? Of course. But they also need to be humble enough to recognize that others' views are useful, too. Do leaders need to persevere when times get tough? Yes. But they also need to recognize when times change and a new direction is called for."*
>
> —**RICHARD L. HUGHES, ROBERT C. GINNETT,** *and* **GORDON J. CURPHY,**
> Leadership: Enhancing the Lessons of Experience

At the 2001 International Entrepreneur Of The Year Conference, Michael Dell—CEO of Dell Computers and the 1989 Entrepreneur Of The Year—spoke about flexibility as a saving grace. "Entrepreneurs have to be willing to fail," he said. "It's very difficult to think up a strategy that's going to anticipate all manner of industry change and evolution. You have to be willing to evolve and be flexible. The faster you make those mistakes and learn from them, the better off you are."

This kind of effort is called "adaptive work," and getting it done takes persistence and bravery. In *The Real Work of Leaders,* Donald L. Laurie cautions: "Adaptive work lies at the core of a company's ability to succeed. Because it often requires new ideas and attitudes that compete with established values, how-ever, it calls for learning the new and unlearning the old."

These rapid shifts make the business environment more precarious and risky. Many dangers, however, come from within your organization rather than from without in the form of complacency. Particularly in large, successful organizations, leaders and employees come to think they have been doing things the right way because their approach has worked so well in the past. The danger resides in ignoring the changing marketplace, which is what IBM did when it ignored the rise of the personal computer and spent several years trying to recoup. Once you fall behind, it is very difficult to get back on track, Laurie says.

The business world is intensely competitive, and you can easily fall behind another company's swift research and development. "The real work of leaders . . . is to create the conditions that enable the whole workforce to adapt to change and to participate in solving the problems that organizations face."

A business can be humming along but hit a sour note if the competitive landscape shifts or market changes make pivotal technologies and business models obsolete. That's when outstanding entrepreneurs rise to the challenge.

Christopher Bergen and Dr. Candace Kendle, 1999 finalists for the Ernst & Young Entrepreneur Of The Year Award in the health care/life sciences category, provide an example. In the mid-1980s, they launched Kendle International, a firm that provides clinical research trials for large pharmaceutical companies. In the early 1990s, however, managed health care changed the drug development industry.

Companies such as Kendle International had to cut costs and development time while simultaneously running more trials. In addition, the company had to provide new and more complex services to its customers, which meant acquiring expertise, technology, and capital so it could become a larger player in the industry.

While transforming itself, the company developed custom software for managing patient data and handling clinical test results. These applications gave Kendle a competitive advantage, because it allowed the firm to provide its customers with more accurate, timelier access to clinical trial information. Today, Kendle's technological capabilities, including its proprietary software and in-house e-learning curriculum, are critically important competitive measures that differentiate it from other contract research organizations.

Judges also assess the processes that Entrepreneur Of The Year nominees set up to adapt to change in their companies, and they examine the way firms establish a culture that encourages and awards creativity.

The Entrepreneur Of The Year judges have empirical evidence that, individual by individual, Entrepreneur Of The Year winners want to foster innovation. The Kauffman Center for Entrepreneurial Leadership studied Entrepreneur Of The Year Award winners to identify the leading practices followed by 906 CEOs from the Entrepreneur Of The Year Academy. The study, which demonstrates that entrepreneurs depend on adaptation, originality, and creativity to make their business grow, showed that many of the respondents typically expand their annual revenues by offering new products and services. If they weren't being creative about going forward, many of them would be merely standing still.

New products are often the highway to corporate growth. The late Ely Callaway, 1994 National Master Entrepreneur Of The Year, abandoned his retirement to reacquire his firm, the Callaway Golf Company. The business was profitable, but Callaway was convinced he could offer better products and increase the company's profits. His first innovation appeared in 1988: a new set of golf clubs with irons that featured a revolutionary new design. More original designs followed until 1990, when Callaway introduced a tremendous hit, the Big Bertha, a new line of oversized woods. The outsized drivers helped golfers hit straighter, longer shots.

By the end of the 1992 golf season, Big Bertha drivers were number one on the Senior Professional Golf Association (PGA) Tour, the Ladies Professional Golf Association Tour (LPGA), and the Nike (then called the Hogan) Tour. With the introduction of Big Berthas, Callaway drove his company—which he had now owned on the second go-round for a decade—into a stage of hypergrowth. His commitment to innovation scored a hole in one.

Most people don't like being compelled to accept and adapt to change per se. They find security in routine and work to avoid uncertainty whenever possible. But a special few find change exciting and challenging. They are inspired by the possibility of doing things new ways. And because they are entrepreneurs, they rally the resources they need to adapt and turn change to their advantage. They know, as Peggy Holman and John Devane write in *The Change Handbook,* that "change is an essential part of life.

"Whatever organization you work in, change is the one thing you can count on. But in the past, change occurred at a predictable and incremental rate. Today, it occurs much more quickly, presenting a challenge for managers. To keep up, managers must learn to be effective change agents.

"In Western society, we've been raised to believe that chaos is bad—it's being out of control. Chaos can be frightening because the outcomes are unpredictable," they write. "Yet, chaos is home to creativity and innovation. Letting go of what's known frees us to create something new.

BEST BUY

Richard Schulze, the 1999 Entrepreneur Of The Year, transformed a small audio components store into a chain of eight stores and then turned the small chain into a big one: the Best Buy Company with 1,700 retail stores under such popular names as Best Buy, Magnolia Hi-Fi, Media Play, On Cue, Sam Goody, and Suncoast.

Schultze's first store almost failed, and he rescued it by turning the tragedy of a hurricane into a "blowout" sale to move his remaining merchandise. Then, after 15 profitable years, Schultze's Sound of Music retail chain again was struggling. Schultze realized that his target population of young males was getting smaller, so he decided to change his product offerings and advertising approach. He risked bankruptcy to set up a store that "applied and embellished the superstore strategy, using a blend of product categories that appealed to both sexes and to an extended range of customers."

Schultze's Best Buy stores were a stunning success until his previously successful methods stopped working, and he had to adapt his mass retailing strategy. By the late 1980s, Best Buy was stumbling. Competition was coming from copycat stores and legendary retailers such as Sears and Montgomery Ward. In addition, price cutting was leading to falling profits. Schultz was up to the challenge. He applied marketing psychology by changing the "look and feel" of his stores and restructuring services to make his customers' experience more enjoyable. For example, he ended the practice of paying commissions to salespeople. Schulze's strategy paid off, most of all because it actually cost less to operate the business under his new plan. Of course, Schulze has continued to innovate by keeping his vision flexible and his eyes open to changes in the world around him.

The biggest test of his ability to pull his company out of trouble happened in 1997 and 1998, when he presided over one of the most dramatic, quickest recoveries in modern retailing. Schultz acknowledges that his second turnaround—heroic as it was—was necessitated by poor management practices and sparked by a major misstep over ordering and subsequently incurring too much debt. In anticipation of a busy 1996 Christmas season, Schulze decided to borrow heavily so he could add a whopping $300 million in additional inventory, most of it computers. Meanwhile, news spread about the launch of Intel's new multimedia Pentium chip. The timing couldn't have been worse. Best Buy found itself buried under a mountain of obsolete PCs.

But that wasn't all. Behind the scenes, Best Buy was cutting prices too low, its inventory controls were woefully insufficient, its operations were cumbersome and its accountability was too loose. Debt was out of control— even in 1995, it stood at $271 million, 72 percent of equity.

At the 1997 Best Buy annual meeting, angry shareholders clamored for Schulze's resignation, but Schulze won the opportunity to try to make a difference in Best Buy's performance.

He adapted everything to Best Buy's new reality, from marketing to midmanagement and inventory controls. He abandoned the chain's famous "No, No, No" pricing strategy: no money down, no monthly payment, no interest, which analysts said had translated into no profit. Schulze shifted Best Buy's merchandise mix away from low-margin items, such as VCRs and computers, and toward more popular, more profitable goods, including software, home appliances, and office furniture. With much regret, he replaced his largely "homegrown" management team with 40 new vice presidents, mostly people he recruited and brought in from outside the company.

Adapting is always hard, and these modifications were harder than most, but Schulze's new strategies worked. Earnings for fiscal year 1998 rose to $94.5 million, a 5,500 percent increase above 1997. By taking a hard look at what had happened and opening himself up to what could be, Schulze saved the day—and not for the first time in a career full of drama—by being creative and, most of all, flexible in the face of change.

Today, according to its Web site, Best Buy is the United States's largest volume specialty retailer of consumer electronics, personal computers, entertainment software, and appliances. From its Eden Prairie, Minnesota, headquarters, Best Buy Company, Inc. (NYSE: BBY) operates retail stores in 41 states and is on track to have more than 550 stores nationwide by 2004. The company operates retail stores and commercial Web sites under the following names: Best Buy (BestBuy.com), Magnolia Hi-Fi, Media Play (MediaPlay.com), On Cue (OnCue.com), Sam Goody (SamGoody.com), and Suncoast (Suncoast.com). The company reaches consumers through nearly 2,000 retail stores nationwide, in Puerto Rico, and in the United States Virgin Islands.

The chain, which posts its mission statement online, has created a substantial online business that is supported by more than 350 United States distribution centers. The mission statement reads: "We improve people's lives by making technology and entertainment products affordable and easy to use."

In the firm's annual report, Schulze writes: "Our leadership team shares a vision for the Company of meeting consumers at the intersection of technology and life. In fiscal 2001, we concluded that this vision required us to look beyond our large format strategy, which attracts primarily techno-savvy, fairly young and predominantly male consumers."

Then he explains yet a third round of innovations and restructuring. "After 35 years of outstanding growth, we needed new distribution channels. We saw an opportunity to reach other large segments of consumers who seek technology products and services that make their time more fun and more productive. We also were challenged to look outside our national borders for new markets in which to open stores. To fuel our long-term growth, we needed to launch our next stage of growth prior to exhausting the opportunity within our large format strategy."

To meet that need, Best Buy acquired Musicland, a music and movie retailer that provides the firm with 1,300 stores and improved access to female consumers, teenagers, and people in rural areas. Deciding to share "best practices and achieve economies of scale with Best Buy," the company also acquired Magnolia Hi Fi, a retailer of high-end consumer electronics, and moved into the Canadian market. Initially, it will have 15 stores in the Toronto area, but Schulze projects 60 to 65 stores across Canada.

He writes: "These strategic initiatives provide us with substantial building blocks for growth. Through these three strategies, we have added new branded retail outlets, mall and rural store formats, a high-end electronic sales and service format, and hundreds of millions of new consumer touch points. We see significant opportunity to extend our retailing leadership in technology and entertainment into new spaces."

Going back to entrepreneurial basics, Schulze discusses how results of these initiatives will be measured. Then he notes: "These key strategies are possible because of our energetic, highly skilled and driven employees. I view them as a competitive advantage.

"In addition . . . we have the executive talent in place to pursue each new initiative while continuing to grow our Best Buy stores and reaching the full potential of these stores. I understand the value of developing a deep bench of skilled leaders and also appreciate the opportunity to focus on what I most enjoy: working with our team to advance our vision, identify strategic growth opportunities and develop the business."

Even after three major innovations, Richard Schulze is still looking for advancement, growth, and development.

"The current situation is this: The environment is more turbulent, we are deluged with information, change applied through one area of expertise no longer works, and the people part of change is difficult to address. The implication is that it's time to systematically include people in the change process and build their capacity for handling turbulence."

The message is clear: Companies that cannot anticipate change and adapt to it are haunted by the possibility of chaos instead of being challenged by the possibility of innovation and adaptation or motivated by the need to anticipate the inevitability of change and plan ahead.

Judge William Saito tells the puzzling saga of a company that did not look ahead. The company had created and successfully marketed "what was supposed to be a phenomenal battery" for operating golf carts. "The batteries were good technology and the business looked good from the perspective of golf carts. But when I talked to the entrepreneurs about their plans and visions for the future, they didn't have any. They weren't looking ahead in terms of wheelchairs, cars, and other vehicles. For me, it was sad to see."

EOY judges almost unanimously identify Richard Schulze of Best Buy, the 1999 Entrepreneur Of The Year, as the epitome of an adaptive entrepreneurial leader who successfully reinvents his vision and his business to stay on top. Schulze, a true cat with nine lives, has been through several transformations. He demonstrates valuable lessons about adaptation along the way, as he continually reshaped his company to meet new demands.

Richard Schulze has continued to innovate by keeping his vision flexible and his eyes open to changes in the world around him.

As Best Buy illustrates, flexibility is critically important. Judge Rebecca Smith points out: "Every good entrepreneur lives life with a damn good Plan B. If someone thinks that everything works according to Plan A, then they don't get it. It comes down to agility, to being able to shift gears as you keep focused while watching the different indicators. It's like bringing a ship into dock. You have to adjust constantly to shifts in the wind and compensate to make sure you stay right on target."

Judge Saito agrees: "Entrepreneurs must understand that their ideas may require some adjustments given the market-place or [the influence of] technology. They must be flexible and adjust and have the diligence to understand what their weaknesses are. They must make modifications to their ideas to make them fit the world right now."

Judge Jack Stack likes to see entrepreneurs broaden their horizon, adapt, and diversify their business—but for a different reason. "You need more than one program, need to be in more than one market, need to deal with more than one commodity. It will help you out when times are bad and it will give you places to grow."

The 2001 Entrepreneur Of The Year, Dr. Phillip Frost, is the founder of the $1 billion IVAX Corporation and knows all about adaptability and planning for growth through diversity. After he sold his first company, Frost acquired a 50 percent interest in a specialty chemical company. Simultaneously, he was working with a former student on a proposal to buy a diagnostics business. He had also started a new pharmaceuticals company from scratch with no sales but with the idea of developing products. Frost combined all three ventures to create IVAX, headquartered in Miami.

In adapting to a changing global marketplace, Frost leveraged IVAX's diversity by using the proceeds from selling brand-equivalent prescription drugs to fund the development of proprietary products. Frost explains that "the success of our generic drugs provided the cash flow that allowed us to invest in proprietary products."

Today, the IVAX holding company includes several operating units, employs 5,800 people, and has subsidiaries in 30 countries. The subsidiaries are engaged in the research, development, manufacture, and marketing of branded and brand-equivalent pharmaceuticals in the United States and international markets. IVAX has subsidiaries specializing in generic drugs, oncology, respiratory therapy (where its development of CFC-free inhalers address one area of growing global environmental concerns), nutraceuticals, and veterinary products.

Frost combined his medical knowledge and his ability to adapt to the market with an entrepreneurial spirit and business acumen to build IVAX Corporation into a pharmaceutical powerhouse. In the process, he helped make affordable, state-of-the-art medical care available to millions of people worldwide. His strategy: "Keep it simple, and go for the developments that will have large-scale implications."

CHALLENGES AND ENDURANCE

"How well did those people ride out the tough times? When other companies were failing, why did they succeed? Either because the owners made the right decisions, or they became more inventive— coming up with new ways to do things so they could make it through."

—JUDGE SUE BURNETT

The challenges that entrepreneurs encounter and the changes they have to make to overcome difficulty make a big impact on the Entrepreneur Of The Year judges. They are aware that entrepreneurs must overcome barriers to entry, that they must defeat difficult circumstances, and that they must prevent, or recover from, corporate disasters. An entrepreneur's ability to meet these challenges is evaluated using a measurement the judges call "degree of difficulty."

Judge Victoria Jackson explains: "I'm particularly interested in assessing the degree of difficulty an entrepreneur overcame. The playing field is never level. For instance, you might see companies where the founders could rely on inherited wealth or already had the capital to acquire or start a company. But the stories that really tug at my heart show personal strength, where someone just put it all on the line. Maybe the entrepreneur sold or mortgaged his or her house. Maybe the entrepreneur began as an immigrant who didn't speak the language and had to learn this culture and scrap it out, or perhaps we're looking at people who had to find a way to persuade others that their ideas were worthy of consideration."

Judge Robert Vukovich assesses degree of difficulty this way: "Let's say I am looking at an entrepreneur who inherited a chemical company and this entrepreneur built it from $10 million in sales to $100 million. I'd definitely put this candidate into the running. Then say I look at somebody who started with nothing and built a $10 million dollar company from scratch with a technological breakthrough. Even though the first company is making more money, that doesn't mean for me that the first deserves better recognition. In fact, it may be the opposite."

Facilitator Carl Thoma believes that entrepreneurs who devise "a strategy that allows them to do well when other people aren't doing as well" or who make their business grow when others aren't growing have "figured out a more innovative way to make something happen."

When judges assess the degree of difficulty entrepreneurs face as they launch a business and manage it over time, they place a premium on the achievements of entrepreneurs whose savvy has been tested by challenges that would discourage most other people. Over the years, judges have seen many examples of unusual challenges that have tested entrepreneurs.

The judges speak from experience. Entrepreneur Of The Year winners, such as Rebecca Smith, Michael Dell, and Paul

Sarvardi, started and developed their businesses during times of economic depression or market instability. Other winners and now judges, such as Steve Papermaster and Ed Iaccobucci, the founder of Citrix Systems, lived through sagas reminiscent of the biblical competition between David and Goliath.

OVERCOMING BARRIERS TO ENTRY

"How much are you ready to sweat? How much stress can you bear to save your company? What kind of commitment do you have? Are you different from most people who would throw in the towel and give up?"

—JUDGE MILTON GRIEF

Entrepreneur Of The Year judges empathize in particular with those who overcome entry barriers, particularly entrepreneurs from minority groups, those with special handicaps, or those laboring under difficult societal circumstances, all of whom work every day to extinguish prejudice and surmount blockades.

Judges Steve Papermaster and Victoria Jackson add that a nominee's personal history is important in their assessments of the degree of difficulty the person has surmounted, particularly when barriers to entry are involved.

According to judge Papermaster: "It's a factor if you take people who came over from China or India and you drop them in the middle of the United States and see what they are able to pull off. This is especially true when you compare them to someone who is a native, who speaks English, who has networks and resources, and who pulls off the same thing."

*A*t the national judging level is where we start to see more competition on the criteria of innovation and originality. We come across several candidates who might have started certain niches in an industry or might have been premier forerunners, but not necessarily founders, of the industry they are in.

—**SUE BURNETT**, *Coowner & President of the Burnett Companies Consolidated*

Sue Burnett founded Choice Staffing in Dallas and Burnett Staffing Specialists in Houston, Austin, El Paso, and San Antonio. Her offices provide temporary and contract staffing and direct hire placements in the areas of administrative support, accounting, law, information technology, human resources, sales, teleskills, electronic assembly, and light industrial.

Burnett's company has been recognized by the *Houston Business Journal* as the largest direct hire placement service, fifth largest temporary service, and sixth largest woman-owned business in Houston. Burnett was also named the "Top Woman Business Owner" by the National Association of Women Business Owners.

She serves on the board of directors of the American Staffing Association, the Arthritis Foundation, Better Business Bureau, and Goodwill Industries.

Judge Jackson imagines herself in the entrepreneur's shoes: "How do I come to a strange country? How do I learn the language? How do I get to a point when I say, 'I can do this.'" Carlos and Jorge de Cespedes of Pharmed Group are a classic example. Jackson recalls their commitment during the start-up phase of their company, which today is the largest independent distributor of medical, surgical, and pharmaceutical supplies. The de Cespedes brothers started their company in an impoverished area characterized by a high rate of unemployment.

Judge Jackson explains that they purchased a company that was losing a significant amount of money and was operating in a highly regulated industry. Just after they acquired the company, state regulations were enacted that made the situation worse. The brothers kept the company going and, at the same time, fought the new legislation all the way to the state's supreme court. The court reversed the ruling that had established the new regulations, and the entrepreneurial team could then reposition the company to take advantage of this new opportunity. In addition, Pharmed Group created a significant number of new jobs in its neighborhood. Jackson believes that less committed leaders might have failed or made do with the restrictive regulatory environment without fighting to improve it.

Entrepreneur Of The Year judges, who are charged with selecting winners who become role models of exceptional enterprise, cannot resist honoring rags-to-riches journeys like the saga of Carlos and Jorge de Cespedes. Certainly, their entrepreneurial skill and energy have been uniquely tested and proven as they overcame substantial entry barriers, including poverty and language, to build a successful international company.

The judges consider how entrepreneurs display ingenuity in overcoming these and other entry barriers, including such industry-specific barriers as restrictive regulations, preexisting market leaders, or entrenched suppliers and such situational barriers as lack of access to financing or a negative regulatory environment. As judge Robert Vukovich affirms: "Barriers to entry are a very important factor when a judge considers whether or not an entrepreneur lives up to the EOY title."

John Bello, for example, got high marks for how he started his company in the face of established competitors and closed distribution networks and other barriers to entry in the soft drink business.

Bello, the 2001 Retail Entrepreneur Of The Year, launched South Beach Beverages, commonly known as SoBe, and created an entirely new category in a business already filled with competitors. In 1996, SoBe established the "healthy refreshment" beverage category when it introduced nutrient-enhanced beverages. Consumers, whom Bello credits as "a lot more sophisticated than many believe," loved SoBe's unique drinks. He took a chance because he believed that consumers would like refreshing, tasty beverages that also deliver needed nutrients.

"We live by a pretty simple motto," Bello says. "Make a little money, have a little fun."

Bello had a long road to success. as he tried to build brand staying power in a crowded field and jump into tight, established distribution networks. To overcome the challenge, Bello set about creating a demand for his product through "buzz marketing" based on word of mouth. He spent most of his marketing budget "at the grass roots level"—at sporting and entertainment events, parties, and trade shows—where people were having fun. "Typical advertising would give us one identity that would exclude different user groups," Bello explains.

"We wanted to have an interactive brand early on so that when people bought our product, they could relate to it in different ways." Bello risked innovative packaging to attract attention and infuse the SoBe brand with personality. His bottles' unique design, complete with the trademark "chasing lizard" logo and witty "lizard line" slogans, stands out on market shelves. The company, which has since been acquired by PepsiCo, Inc., now sells 30 varieties of healthy beverages. Bello used creativity and originality to knock down barriers to entry.

Dell Computer's Michael Dell, the first person to ever be awarded Ernst & Young's National Entrepreneur Of The Year title, also encountered entry barriers when he and his executive team set out in October 1987 to seek outside financing. He recalls: "We went out a week after the stock market crash. Then the week of our road show, *Business Week* published an article saying the computer business was going to fall apart and this 'Dell thing' was a fad that wasn't going to work. It said nobody would buy computers directly from the manufacturer, that you need to have stores . . . you know, steeped in the conventional wisdom and thinking. It made for interesting questions during the road show because, generally, if you put something in magazines, people believe it. So we had to overcome all that."

And they did. Dell and his team raised $20 million in initial funding and another $50 million when they went public nine months later. In fact, Dell's early supporters have been handsomely rewarded for their investment. Anyone who bought Dell stock during its IPO and kept it has received a staggering 26,000 percent return.

Dell is renowned for revolutionizing the PC and computing world by serving customers directly and by providing build-to-order (and therefore, low inventory) machines. When he talked about his innovation on a video created for the 2001 Entrepreneur Of The Year Awards gathering, Dell explained that other, unintended breakthroughs occurred. "I saw an incredible opportunity to create direct relationships with the customers. But when I started the company, I didn't know the incredible advantage we had. For example, we had such great information from customers that we could build a logistics and information system that gave us a profound advantage in terms of cost of materials, transformation costs, and lower cycle time. That meant lower working capital and we could extend into other markets and geographies."

Dell says that as the company gains information, he likes to have "eurekas" all the time. "It's sort of a discovery every day; we learn a little more about the opportunity we have in front of us, how far the industry can grow, and how much we can extend it."

Clearly, Dell and his executives spent time educating potential investors. As judge Saito explains, teaching the world to understand something new is often a hurdle entrepreneurs must clear: "It's part of the job of entrepreneurs to evangelize and educate the world to understand their new creation."

Jerry Yang and David Filo, founders of Yahoo!, and Tim Koogle, Yahoo!'s first CEO and president, know something about educating the marketplace. In 1995 they made a catalog of Web sites and turned it into the first online navigational guide to the Internet. They pioneered the Internet portal business. By the time the Yahoo! trio became national finalists for the 1998 Entrepreneur Of The Year Award for Internet products and services, Yahoo! served 15 million users a day and collected revenues of $67 million. Today, Yahoo! Inc. is the top Internet brand globally and reaches the largest Internet audience worldwide. Over the years, Yahoo!'s leadership won the confidence of venture capitalists and stock market investors and at the same time forged a first-of-its-kind Web platform of multimedia communications, content, marketing, and commercial services.

But Yahoo!'s leaders had to first clear the start-up gate before anyone ever heard of a portal. That's why judge Sue Burnett always considers a firm's entire start-up challenge. She wants to know if starting out was "a breeze" or difficult. She considers how the nominee's business was financed, noting that some entrepreneurs have to take greater risks than others by funding their ventures with personal credit cards and borrowing against their family's home. She adds: "We saw several people with financial partners who just supplied them endlessly with money—they never had any degree of difficulty."

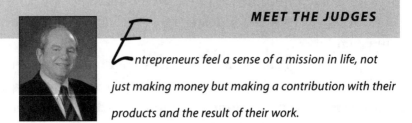

Entrepreneurs feel a sense of a mission in life, not just making money but making a contribution with their products and the result of their work.

—**FEDERICO SANCHEZ**, *President of Interlink Development Counselors*

Since 1977, Federico Sanchez has been president of Interlink Development Counselors, based in Puerto Rico. Interlink specializes in residential and resort communities and mixed-use projects in the middle- to high-income range. As Sanchez explains, "A key ingredient of our success has been to define niches and opportunities that others don't follow. We create a market where others say it doesn't exist. For instance, we can handle urban renewal projects, which others cannot, because we bring originality to the architecture, consideration of the surrounding area, and quality construction."

Before Interlink, Sanchez worked as a project engineer and project manager with an American construction company and was stationed throughout the Caribbean and South America. Over the years, he has served as both vice president and president of several development companies and garnered experience in residential construction, resort development, commercial properties, and land development.

During his career, Sanchez has been affiliated with many professional and civil organizations, some of which are the National Association of REALTORS®, Recreational Development Council of Urban Land Institute, and the board of governors of United Way. Sanchez has also taught at the University of Puerto Rico's School of Business and was a trustee of the University of the Sacred Heart for seven years.

PHARMED

Carlos and Jorge de Cespedes, 2001 national finalists for the Ernst & Young Entrepreneur Of The Year Award in the health sciences category, established and now manage a $400+ million medical products firm. As the award judges discovered, the achievements of the de Cespedes brothers are much greater than the jobs they've created and the products they distribute in the United States and Latin America. Life began testing their ability to overcome difficulties when they were still children.

In 1960, Carlos, age 11, and Jorge, age 8, arrived in Miami from Cuba as part of a secret exodus of children known as Operation Pedro Pan. While living in a holding camp, the boys saved their weekly allowance of $1.40—which they received on the condition that they write a letter home—and also the money Jorge collected from writing letters for other kids. By the time the boys were reunited with their parents six years later, Jorge had saved $1,500.

Twenty years after they landed in Florida, the de Cespedes brothers left their executive positions with SmithKline Beecham Laboratories and started Pharmed in 1980 with $500, an answering machine, and a newspaper ad. They chose the Caribbean and Latin America as their main markets. Within two years, their sales had reached $1.7 million—and they've never stopped growing. They leased their first warehouse in 1983 and brought sales to $3.1 million. They became Johnson & Johnson's Florida distributor and opened operations in Panama City, Panama, in 1985 and took sales to $6 million. Pharmed earned its first major hospital contract in 1986 and had nine major hospital contracts by 1991, when sales reached $31 million.

In 1994, Pharmed constructed an 80,500-square-foot headquarters and distribution facility and was recognized by *Hispanic Business Magazine* as the "Fastest Growing Hispanic Company in the USA."

In 1995, the de Cespedes brothers hired several experienced senior executives and installed a state-of-the-art computer system to handle larger contracts. A year later they established Pharmed Costa Rica, added long-term care products, and brought sales to $44.8 million. By the end of 1998, sales reached $62 million and Pharmed carried 55 private label products. The company continued to grow with alliances in Latin America and the founding of Pharmed Brazil, and 1999 sales were estimated to be $80 million.

The Pharmed Group currently distributes more than 25,000 products and has expanded into manufacturing vitamins and private-label brands. The company's evolution includes the introduction of pharmaceutical-grade olive oil and the expansion of both its distribution network and its manufacturing capacity. The Pharmed Group currently distributes more than 25,000 products, including pharmaceutical and medical supplies; oncology, generic, and brand name drugs; veterinary supplies; hospital products; and physical and occupational therapy products.

In 2001, Pharmed, which is now a $400 million company, won the prestigious Cutting Edge Award, which is given to the Florida company that exemplifies the finest innovative business techniques and marketing and sales strategies as well as management strength and entrepreneurship. That same year, it won a regional Ernst & Young Entrepreneur Company of the Year Award in the medical category.

The de Cespedes brothers turned their successes into community contributions to help educate and care for other people. They support a medical clinic to serve low-income and immigrant families and scholarships for their employees' children. They also support a Cuban American studies program at the University of Miami and at Florida International University.

The company's Web site explains that with their products clients "get one asset that cannot be purchased: dedication. From the senior management team, to the customer service representatives taking orders, Pharmed Group has a depth of product knowledge that assures the client unparalleled service." The company's mission statement is clear:

> This is who we are;
> This is what we stand for;
> This is what we are all about;

This is the core ideology of our company:

The purpose of our company: To create an environment ideal for incubating entrepreneurial processes. This company will forever nourish products and services toward improving human life.

Our responsibilities are:

To our employees

To our customers

To society at large

To the stockholders

OVERCOMING ADVERSITY

"How much are you ready to sweat? How much stress can you bear to save your company? What kind of commitment do you have? Are you different from most people who would throw in the towel and give up?"

—JUDGE MILTON GRIEF

Never say never. Entrepreneurs must believe in themselves and persevere if they aspire to build a high-growth and long-lasting business. First of all, simply being an entrepreneur and starting a new business is an inherently difficult thing to do.

After all, entrepreneurs have to be realists, and as John L. Nesheim acknowledges in *High Tech Start Up*, daunting personal costs can be part of an entrepreneurial venture. Personal costs include increased stress; strained relationships; working around the clock; a lack of backup staff; less time for health and fitness; increased psychological pressure; the need to handle make-or-break decisions quickly; a heightened awareness of the risk of failure; increased pressure to succeed; and a sharp increase in personal introspection. Many start-up founders, he notes, find themselves asking, "Why am I doing this? Will this give me personal and professional fulfillment?" Those are difficult life-altering questions each entrepreneur must answer alone, although the judges are aware of these tensions because they, too, have survived this process.

As the judges can testify, entrepreneurs almost always encounter challenges, including those that threaten their business. Sometimes stubborn force of will is your best weapon, a steadfast refusal to accept the dictates of prevailing wisdom until you have exhausted every alternative.

Judge Robert Vukovich, the successful entrepreneur behind Wellspring Pharmaceutical Corporation, once teetered on the brink of bankruptcy, but he never folded nor did he stop seeking relationships and results that could build his success.

He recalls a time, when starting up one of his first pharmaceutical companies, that things were not going according to plan. "I was almost bankrupt. I sold my boat. I took out a second mortgage on my house. I was up to my ears in credit card debt. I had three kids to put through school, and I was still going forward like a dope." Sure, Vukovich knew he was taking a big risk, but he says that it never even occurred to him that he would fail. Today, Vukovich is very happy that he was so stubbornly committed and took a risk on his dream. "I turned the corner; some cash flowed in; things began to click; I got some business partners and a couple of drugs approved; and bingo! I had a $200 million company."

Where others might have faltered, Vukovich prevailed. Perhaps his comment that it never even occurred to him that he might fail reveals that succeeding can be as much about psychology as about informed decision making. For example, facilitator Carl Thoma and judges such as Jack Stack and Federico Sanchez mention a well-known phenomenon among entrepreneurs: they don't see obstacles, only opportunities.

When judge Stack evaluates an entrepreneur, he looks for endurance; he wants to know that a company is going to last. That's not always predictable because entrepreneurs can encounter any number of unexpected challenges.

Judges examine the tough times discussed in nominees' applications to see how each entrepreneur overcame obstacles and if he or she used every skill—from strategic planning to team building—at hand. Surmounting difficult situations can depend on innovative problem solving or sheer determination, including the refusal to take no for an answer.

Judge William Saito cautions: "If you bet the farm, you're going to have very stressful days. But I think if you believe in yourself and you believe you are doing something truly substantial, those beliefs can lead you through an extremely trying time."

Judge Rebecca Smith, too, has learned that having "passion for what you're doing . . . [gives you] almost a superhuman ability to continue to conquer in the face of certain defeat. So if you are doing and pursuing, everything falls into place." Or as she says in short, "When no is not the right answer, don't let no be the answer."

Smith heard plenty of no's in her day, especially when, at 29, she decided to start a construction business. "When I took the step of starting my own company, there were all kinds of reasons against it. The market was down, construction was slowing, big companies were laying off, and interest rates were going through the roof. There were any number of reasons why I should not have started a company," explains Smith.

She doesn't even mention that she was boldly venturing into a man's world. One of her longtime colleagues reports: "In the early years of company growth, most potential clients looked at her as though she had two heads, wondering what a woman was doing in the hard-hat world of commercial construction." Smith states that she simply wouldn't "validate" the bias: "By never acknowledging the attitude, I set it aside and never made it real."

Before facing customers, Smith cut her teeth dealing with negativity from bankers. As soon as she saw a banker, usually a man, start shifting in his seat and looking as though he were about to say no, Smith wouldn't let it happen. "I wouldn't let the individual say it. Or if somehow he slipped out a no, I would never leave the meeting saying, 'I understand. Thank you for your time.' Instead I would say, 'Apparently, I have not provided you with adequate information because if I had, you would not be coming to the conclusion that you've come to. So let me go back and pull everything together and come back to your office in two or three days.'"

Smith describes her persistence as more than the famous entrepreneurial optimism: "It is optimism based on the certainty that everybody else just doesn't get it." Eventually, Smith found people who "got it" and today her company, A.D. Morgan Corporation, has a reputation for exceptional construction management and general contractor services. According to Smith, the secret to overcoming adversity and succeeding: "Believe in yourself."

Judge Joanna Lau of Lau Technologies looks for an entrepreneur's ability to handle difficulties such as Smith faced. "It's easy to start a business, but along the way there are a lot of different obstacles. The thing that stands out with me is how an entrepreneur overcomes obstacles."

MEET THE JUDGES

When I judge entrepreneurs, I don't just look at the name brand or how much money they make. I want to read a story that will influence our next generation of entrepreneurs. I want to see entrepreneurs who are different, with stories that stand out.

—**JOANNA T. LAU**, *Chairman and CEO of LAU Technologies*

Joanna T. Lau is founder and CEO of LAU Technologies, a management consulting and investment company. Her mission is to fund and foster new ideas and companies. In 1990 Joanna acquired a small defense manufacturing company and has grown it into three business units providing systems integration, development, and delivery of high-end electronic systems for military applications and for secure identification and surveillance systems.

In 1996 LAU spun out one of its divisions, Viisage Technology, and took it public. Viisage serves the secure identification industry and provides driver's license systems in 13 states utilizing the patented facial recognition technology. The LAU Security Systems develops and deploys the latest patented "Face in the Crowd" facial recognition technologies serving federal, intelligence, and foreign communities. Another LAU subsidiary, LAU Defense Systems, serves the defense industry with its design and development of electronic control systems and is the third largest VME designer and manufacturer in the world.

Lau has received numerous business honors in addition to her Ernst & Young Award, including numerous awards and recognition from the United States Army, Prime Contractors, and the Small Business Administration.

She is on the board of directors of the John F. Kennedy Library Foundation, is a member of the Army Science Board, and is a trustee of the National Defense Industrial Association. She is on the board of directors of BostonFed Bankcorp, Inc., is a trustee of Bryant College, and is an overseer of

Northeastern University. Lau is also a member of the Young President's Organization, the Committee of 200, and the International Women's Forum.

As an entrepreneur, you need to be ready to face and overcome the prospect of failure. In *The Guru Guide to Entrepreneurship,* the late Wilson Harrell, founder of almost 100 companies and past publisher of *Inc.* magazine, compares the feeling of facing failure to his experiences as a fighter pilot during World War II. He was shot down behind enemy lines and had to stay buried in a cornfield for 11 days, breathing through a hose in his mouth. After conquering the fear he felt, he gained a sense of being truly alive.

Drawing on your internal courage helps you take risks, persevere after problems erupt, and learn from your failures. Business expert Dennis N.T. Perkins learned many lessons about fear and leadership in the saga of British adventurer Sir Ernest Shackleton's explorations of the Antarctic in 1914 and wrote about them in *Leading at the Edge.* He derived ten principles for confronting difficult situations based on Shackleton's experience leading his men to safety in an incredible and dangerous 312-mile trek.

The advertisement Shackleton ran in English newspapers to recruit sailors for his trip read:

> Men wanted for hazardous journey. Small wages, bitter cold, long months of complete darkness, constant danger, safe return doubtful. Honor and recognition in case of success.

It doesn't sound very encouraging, but thousands of men volunteered for the trip, and Shackleton selected 27. When disaster hit, he had to shift his goal from crossing the continent to getting all his men out alive—and he succeeded in meeting that goal. In the process, as Perkins explains, these are the ten principles for confronting difficult situations derived from Shackleton's experience:

1. Always keep the ultimate goal in mind while you focus your energy on short-term goals. Keep momentum going; cherish even small victories.

2. Use visible and memorable symbols and behaviors to set a personal example. If your company faces difficult times, reassure people calmly with straight talk and resolution to move ahead.

3. Inspire others to feel optimistic and self-confident, yet stay in touch with reality. Shackleton firmly believed he would succeed. That belief and his ongoing positive outlook helped motivate his men. Even while they were stranded, he led a discussion about an expedition to Alaska, which provided a future focus and a promise of other adventures, implying they would triumph over this present calamity.

4. Stay strong; don't feel guilty about taking care of yourself so you can continue to lead. Although you often need to put in long hours, devote great energy to leadership, and show concern for others, take care of yourself, too. Recognize your limits and pull back when you are doing too much, becoming exhausted, or endangering your health.

5. Continually reinforce a message of teamwork to emphasize that you have to stay together to survive.

6. Minimize status differences and emphasize courtesy and mutual respect. Downplay hierarchy during a crisis. Certainly, people recognize the need for legitimate authority and different salaries, roles, and titles. But in-

stead of creating an elite upper class, create an environment of mutual respect and mutual caring.

7. Overcome the strains of conflict by avoiding unnecessary power struggles; engage dissidents and counter anger when it occurs. Diffuse any conflicts early on before they grow. Recognize that disagreement is inevitable in any organization, so manage conflict productively. For instance, encourage team members to admit their differences and identify problems.

8. Find something that everyone can celebrate, laugh about, and enjoy. This approach enables you to break a "spiral of depression," stimulate creativity, and overcome fear and anxiety. Lightening up can help team members refocus and get reenergized about overcoming obstacles.

9. Be willing to take a big risk when necessary. Don't take risks for their own sake or take unnecessary chances, but do take risks when justified. Then, don't hesitate—act decisively.

10. Don't give up, because there is always some further action you can take. "Tenacious creativity" is the ideal; this means looking for alternative possibilities despite the difficulties. When things go wrong, call on the collective creativity of your team to find a solution.

"Winning leaders cultivate the ability to monitor the condition of each person on the team and to sense when individuals are becoming overwhelmed. They need to direct negative energy toward activities that divert people's attention from their problems and harness this energy for positive results," Perkins writes. "Making a friend of fear means developing a way to detoxify the fear so that you can maximize your own effectiveness."

When you feel marooned and your team is starting to panic, think of Sir Ernest Shackleton rescuing all 27 of his men from Antarctica. He kept them focused, united, and energized while camping on ice and eating penguins. Now that's leadership against adversity.

The judges find that overcoming obstacles is an individual journey, but it builds knowledge and wisdom in a hurry. Time and again during these interviews, judges would say something like, "If I knew then what I know now, I never would have gone through with it." And yet they did when they had to.

For example, judge Milton Grief was once confronted with a very big mistake not of his own creation. He could have walked away, but instead he found a solution. Grief had hired a company comptroller who covered up a billing error that amounted to a $500,000 loss in one month. On learning of the mistake, Grief was forced to notify his bank, which had given him a loan. The bank decided to call in its loan and sever its relationship with Grief and his fledgling company, American Fabricators. Grief recalls thinking, "This is your idea, this is your baby. Are you going to give up or are you going to fight to save this thing?"

Grief pledged himself to a "110 percent commitment" to resolve the crisis. "I had to sacrifice some employees' jobs to save others. I had to sell off assets. Every day was a battle. The bank had taken all my cash." Grief also came up with a system in which he would state goals to the bank and, when he met those goals, the bank would release cash for payables.

Eventually, Grief repaid the loan. As he explains, the icing on the cake came when he arrived at the bank with his final payment and was invited by the bank manager to continue as a customer by taking on a new loan, which the bank was prepared to offer. "When the Entrepreneur Of The Year judges looked at my nomination and decided to give me an award, I'm sure that's one of the things they looked at," says Grief.

*A*n entrepreneur has to be able to grow with the company. When you see someone start a company, build it, hire the people, take it public, expand worldwide, and continue to maintain control, that's some kind of entrepreneur.

—**MILTON GRIEF,** Founder and President of American Fabricators Inc. (AFI)

Major long-term contracts at Milton Grief's precision sheet metal fabrication company comprise 80 percent of its business and include orders to produce appliance panels, fenders for cranes, gas pumps, components for computers, and parts for other industries.

To meet customer needs, Grief is continuously evaluating and upgrading his machinery and software to ensure that operations do not become outdated and to provide quick project turnaround. He has also taken the unusual approach of relying on a single manufacturer to supply all equipment, making tools interchangeable and employee training more efficient. "Much like Herb Kelleher at Southwest Airlines, another successful Entrepreneur Of The Year winner," says Grief.

Grief's company has been named Business of the Year by the *Nashville Business Journal.* He serves as chairman of a ten-member planning commission in Brentwood, Tennessee, and is on the finance board of his church.

That kind of resilience is critical for all creative figures, including leaders who experience triumphs and setbacks and must learn to create triumph from setbacks. One key to resilience, says Jeffrey Sonnenfeld, author of "Leading by Resilience," an essay in *The Future of Leadership,* is opting for fight rather than flight; that is, knowing when to "take arms against a sea of troubles."

The successful leader must first become blind to stress and persevere in spite of it. The key is to find a way to direct, or sublimate, the stress that you experience.

Secondly, successful leaders must recruit others and bring in reinforcements. Resilient people use their personal networks to ascend and to recover from setbacks. They rebuild their heroic stature and work to regain the trust and credibility they lost during the setback. Sonnenfeld says that a leader must jump back into the fray to demonstrate the talents that earned greatness in the first place.

Examples include Donald Trump's recovery from an overwhelming debt of $975 million or former junk bond king Michael Milken's victory over prostate cancer and his ability to build more successful enterprises, including a cradle-to-grave learning company. The new mayor of New York City, self-made success Michael Bloomberg, was fired in 1981 from Salomon Brothers, albeit with millions of dollars in severance money that he used to move forward and create his own business. Even Steve Jobs was forced out of Apple, although he returned to take up leadership again two years later.

How did these leading businessmen achieve this reinvention? It suggests that resilient leaders respond to challenges by getting stronger rather than weaker. They triumph over adversity through persistence and creativity. As Nietzsche said, "What does not destroy me makes me stronger." Or as scientist Louis Pasteur said, "Chance favors the mind that's prepared." This means that you should prepare for the setbacks and challenges that no doubt lie ahead. Just consider the tongue-in-cheek maxim that to be successful in life, first you should select great parents. In other words, many things are beyond your control, so control the things you can.

"Solving problems—or, more accurately, enabling others to solve problems—is the leader's real work. By identifying and framing problems, a leader jump-starts the crucial process of marshaling the resources needed to eliminate them," points out Donald L. Laurie in *The Real Work of Leaders.*

Judge Jack Stack, who popularized open-book management, implemented a training program to teach every employee of his SRC Holdings Corporation how to read a corporate balance sheet and how to understand the financial aspects of business. He explains that educating his workforce, most of whom remanufacture engine parts, gives them the means to develop and test their ideas. He believes that, particularly for those with an aptitude in business finance, he has enabled his employees to analyze the feasibility of their ideas and even propose and operate new businesses. In fact, Stack is so confident in his workers that he set up an SRC venture fund to spin off businesses that his employees pitch.

Stack had an experience during his early years at SRC that reassured him his technique for providing financial engineering training to employees was a profitable investment. Just before Christmas in 1986, General Motors abruptly canceled an order for 5,000 engines—an abrupt loss of 40 percent of SRC's business for the following year. Like many business crises, this one was practically unforeseeable and immediately left Stack with an unsavory choice: he had to either lay off 100 people or risk losing the entire company.

Stack talked to salespeople and customers in an effort to chase down new leads. He searched for new business, all to no avail. Layoffs loomed as the only answer and Stack's employees knew it. Firing employees would be a particularly bitter choice for Stack, who takes layoffs personally. "It's a sign of management failure," he says. "You lay people off when you've screwed up." At the brink of the layoff decision, a group of senior employees came to Stack to propose a radical solution.

Capitalizing on the full disclosure available under open-book management, the employees had analyzed the possibility of creating new products to take the place of the engines that would never be built. They proposed that SRC produce replacement engines for the automobile aftermarket. Doing so would mean that SRC would have to tool up and produce more than 100 engine models for 100 different car models on the road. Stack's employees had been careful in their research. Encouraged by the numbers, Stack gave them the go-ahead. In the end, the employees' idea worked. Not only did Stack avoid the layoffs, but he was also able to add 100 new people.

Stack's experience illustrates the fact that, often, handling adversity and obstacles means taking on risk, and that risk can include spending capital and resources to produce 100 different types of engines. But, hey, at least you're still in business. All that's left to deal with is managing, tracking, and increasing your money, which we confront in the next chapter.

CHAPTER SUMMARY

Who doesn't love the entrepreneur-as-Horatio-Alger stories about pushing boundaries, beating the odds, and triumphing in the face of adversity? When entrepreneurs launch a new business or manage it through turbulent times, Entrepreneur Of The Year judges look to see how the entrepreneurs applied innovation to conquer their challenges.

From inspiration to execution, judges look for the evidence and rewards of creative thinking and behaving. They see it in original ideas, products, and services. They see it in how entrepreneurs go up against odds that can have as much to do with the adversities of personal circumstance as with the consequence of mistakes and accidents.

When examining EOY Award nominees, judges have determined there are critical times and critical ways in which an entrepreneur's capabilities as an innovator and a nurturer of innovation are tested. The first is during the launch of a new company, product, or service. The second is when entrepreneurs go up against obstacles or simply set new challenges for themselves and their respective companies. Finally, judges look at whether entrepreneurs have initiated compensation and reward programs to inspire and reinforce creative thinking among employees.

CHAPTER 5

Financial Performance

MONEY MATTERS

"Money is better than poverty, if only for financial reasons."

—WOODY ALLEN

Entrepreneur Of The Year judge Milton Grief tells the story of a friend who started a successful business. Sales were soaring and the friend was "shipping like crazy," Grief recounts. But even as the company's revenues grew, the friend found himself scrambling to pay the bills. Eventually the company failed to meet payroll and the heartbroken entrepreneur was forced to sell the business.

What happened? How could a business that was attracting new customers and rapidly increasing its sales fail so spectacularly? To paraphrase a political cliché: It's the financials, stupid.

Judge Grief's friend was probably like many entrepreneurs who start out with a great idea and limitless energy but with little understanding of the financial elements that ultimately determine the fate of every company. Indeed, judge Grief confirms that in setting up the business model, his friend neglected to consider his accounts receivable. In other words, while the company was signing contracts, delivering products, and booking revenues, no one had thought about how or when it would actually get paid. The friend was shocked to find that his customers were waiting 120 days after delivery to pay their bills. Despite its strong revenues, the company was killed by a cash flow crisis that could have been foreseen and prevented with basic financial management.

Throughout our conversations, the EOY judges consistently identified financial management as both the most critical element in turning a business idea into a viable company and the single most common deficiency among entrepreneurs. This shouldn't be a surprise. The people who come up with the best ideas for new products and services usually aren't accountants or even MBAs. They are people with the ability to spot a market opportunity, the courage to act, and the perseverance to build something out of nothing, but none of those qualities implies an understanding of financial management. Recognizing and seizing a market opportunity at the right time can get a new business off the ground, but to grow and survive, the owner must build on the numbers.

"A lot of entrepreneurs probably don't have the financial background that's needed to take a company forward," judge Grief concludes. "They either know a product or they know a customer, but they have difficulty when watching the numbers."

Of course, financial naïveté is not the exclusive domain of novice entrepreneurs. As proven during the technology bubble of the 1990s, people who should know better sometimes get so carried away with a fresh idea or a new technology that they forget basic financial principles, or at least they convince themselves that details like profits can be put off until later. When musing about the dot-com phenomenon, facilitator Carl Thoma opines that "there has never been a great company built that wasn't financially viable."

Not all dot-com failures were doomed from the start. Many were just spectacular examples of financial mismanagement. The remarkable rise and fall of Webvan, for example, illustrates many of the financial blunders usually reserved for inexperienced entrepreneurs.

At the crest of the Internet wave, Louis Borders, the founder of Borders Books and Music, tried to revolutionize grocery shopping with the creation of Webvan, an Internet site that would deliver online grocery purchases to your door. After attracting millions of private dollars and launching the service in San Francisco, Webvan raised $375 million in its November 1999 initial public offering. By the time Webvan acquired its chief rival, Homegrocer.com, the two online grocers had together raised more than $1 billion and counted some of the venture capital industry's most powerful firms among their investors.

Nevertheless, in July 2001 Webvan announced that it would file for Chapter 11 bankruptcy protection. Was the bankruptcy a surprise? Well, considering that as of January of that year the company had a burn rate of $100 million per quarter and just over $212 million in the bank, it shouldn't have been. It was obviously time to cut costs. But rather than scaling back, Webvan's management continued with the aggressive plans it had conceived in better days. It did this in the face of dwindling growth, mounting losses, and an increasingly unfriendly market for fresh capital.

The moral of the Webvan tale is not that e-commerce is a failure or even that people will never buy groceries online. (Several smaller online delivery services are still in business today.) The true lesson of the tale is that management decisions must be based on a solid understanding of financial realities. As Carl Thoma notes, "Entrepreneurship is not a con game. A smart entrepreneur does financial planning and financial verification and makes sure, from the financial standpoint, that what he's doing is viable. He can't make something for $1.10

and sell it to the world for $1.10, and he can't start selling candy at 50¢ a bar without noticing that somebody across the street is already selling the same candy for 35¢."

WINNERS' MOVES IN FINANCING

"What better way to measure if an entrepreneur is succeeding than to measure financial performance?"

—JUDGE ROBERT VUKOVICH

Entrepreneur Of The Year winners not only understand financials, but they have mastered them and integrated them into their management practices and decisions. Although it's not a requirement, it turns out that every national EOY winner has turned a profit in his or her venture. Such consistent success could not be achieved unless the members of the group each displayed a canny financial sense in addition to the other qualities that we've identified as the keys to their success. A 1997 study revealed three financial practices that characterize the EOY winners.

1. EOY winners obtain financing without giving up control. EOY winners make it a point to find and use financing vehicles that allow them to retain their voting control. As a result, they tend to avoid venture capitalists and many other institutional investors, who inevitably demand a large stake in any business in return for their participation. Although financing sources vary by industry, the majority of EOY winners rely on bank loans, friends, family, staff, and customers for funding. These sources, along with personal savings, represent the traditional means of obtaining start-up or seed money.

What distinguishes EOY winners from many entrepreneurs is that they continue to rely on these sources even after the company becomes established. This determination to retain control is quite impressive when you consider that the need for capital is an almost continuous concern for new businesses. Many would-be entrepreneurs think that financing their company is simply a matter of raising their start-up funds and getting to work. But even after a company's initial start-up costs are covered, there are an infinite number of reasons that subsequent capital infusions will be required. For example, a company that takes off from the start might unexpectedly find itself in need of capital to build up inventories to meet demand. On a less positive but unfortunately more common note, entrepreneurs often overestimate sales growth, a mistake that leaves them short of cash and in need of outside funds.

Cash shortages are not the only reason that some entrepreneurs elect to give up some control over their business. The need for outside expertise, particularly with regard to finance and technology, often motivates entrepreneurs to sacrifice equity in order to bring in outside help. This fact makes it all the more impressive that the EOY winners were able to obtain the funds they needed and wisely use that capital to grow their businesses without giving up control.

2. EOY winners use debt wisely. Even if you insist on retaining control of your company, there's no getting around the fact that growing a business requires capital. EOY winners use debt to finance growth, allowing them to preserve their own equity stakes. The winners often go through multiple rounds of financing, raising fresh capital every two and a half years on average. But even as they take on debt, they are aggressive in planning how they will service it. In particular, EOY winners focus on maintaining margins adequate to finance growth. Our judges reveal that debt in and of itself is not a negative factor in weighing the merits of a given company. Instead, the judges look at a company's overall capital structure, which EOY winners smartly manage by maintaining reasonable debt-to-capital ratios and turning leverage into a critical advantage.

3. EOY winners share the wealth. Selectively granting stock ownership to employees is a common characteristic of management among EOY winners. They may use equity to attract top management or board members; they may also use it as a bonus or incentive for employees. A 2001 study by the Ernst & Young Entrepreneur of the Year Institute and the Kauffman Center for Entrepreneurial Leadership revealed that the ratio of incentives to base salary among a company's employees is a key indicator of firm vitality. Noting that equity compensation is the most important incentive for firm growth, the report concludes that "incentives appear to empower both growth and, to a lesser degree, profitability."

IT ALL STARTS WITH A PLAN

"It's important to show that the business plan and the concepts are in fact very practical and working."

—JUDGE ROBERT VUKOVICH

No matter what growth strategy brought success to the EOY winners, all of these entrepreneurs shared one common trait: they mapped out their strategy in advance with a detailed business plan. Many entrepreneurs seem to think that the business plan is a document whose sole purpose is to attract investors. In seeking to do that, owners draft business plans that have about the same degree of accuracy as their résumés—the facts are probably "legit," but they are massaged in a way that presents the company in the best possible light. When planning for your company's growth, EOY judges advise you to lose that self-promotional mind-set and face reality.

A well-written business plan is important mainly as a reflection of you, the entrepreneur, say Mark Van Osnabrugge and Robert J. Robinson, authors of *Angel Investing*, because most investors do take business plans with a grain of salt.

In fact, venture capitalists say that most of the business plans they see are "just plain bad," according to John L. Nesheim, author of *High Tech Start Up*, who explains that business plans that work focus on three areas:

1. Showing the start-up's distinctive competence

2. Showing the company's competitive advantage

3. Showing management's plan to sustain that advantage

The third item is of utmost importance. Investors want to see more than just technology—they want to see a plan that shows advantage. Nesheim notes that your business plan should include these items:

- *An executive summary.* The purpose of the plan, including the amount of funding needed and how it will be used.

- *Customer need and business opportunity.* The product/service idea proposition.

- *Business strategy and key milestones.* The plan to outmaneuver the competition.

- *Marketing plan.* The company's solution to meet a basic need, the ideal customer proposition, market segment and size, distribution channels, partners, business model, branding, sales strategy, customer support, five-year forecast, competition, and positioning.

- *Operations plan.* Plan for engineering, Web site, manufacturing/outsourcing, faculties, and administration.

- *Management and key personnel.* Organization, staffing plan, detailed résumés of leadership, incentive compensation program, and company culture plan.

- *Financial projections.* Overview and key assumptions, five-year forecasts, income statement, balance sheet, and cash flow statement.

Writing a winning plan is an important part of the process. Develop it yourself; don't hire someone else to do it. When you prepare your plan, keep it short, use solid, plain language, and be specific about your market, according to *Angel Investing.* Use realistic projections and openly address risks and problems. Discuss the firm's financing needs. Show that you understand the investors' needs as well as your own. List possible exit strategies. Show the plan to friends, get advice, and revise, revise, revise.

The business plan is the bedrock of growth management. Your business plan must accurately reflect the current financial condition of your company and must present your best-guess estimates about what the future holds for your company, your employees, your investors, your customers, and your industry. In terms of growth projections, the business plans of new companies should always look to the breakeven point—the point at which the business takes in as much as it pays out. We'll talk more about how start-up companies reach breakeven later in this chapter, but for now the most important thing to remember is that you have to create a business plan that maps out your financial road to the breakeven point, and you have to manage according to that plan every month.

Each month you should track the reality of your sales in comparison with your projections. If there's a shortfall, you should start cutting costs immediately. Don't think that things will get better next month as sales start to roll in; that kind of thinking can be the start of a fatal downward spiral for a young firm. If you find yourself failing to progress toward breakeven, you must act fast. Don't be afraid to modify your plans. As the judges so insightfully advise, don't let your expectations define your strategy; ultimately, the numbers must guide your business decisions. One final caveat from the judges: If you take the steps that the numbers suggest and you're still not making progress, you need to rethink the fundamental premise of your business plan—and maybe your entire business.

UNDERSTANDING YOUR FINANCIAL INDICATORS

"You can be the greatest guy, the greatest innovator, the greatest engineer . . . have charisma, be a great speaker, but you can still be the worst manager because you don't have command of the financials."

—JUDGE JACK STACK

You cannot guide a company's strategic direction without a sound understanding of the financials. Even if an entrepreneur is an expert in his or her industry or a master of the technology that gives a company its competitive advantage, there is no way to assess the past and current performance of any business line without mastering the numbers. Without accurate performance data, it is impossible for you to identify profit drivers or potential areas for cost cutting, and therefore it's impossible to create a strategy for the future.

Simply put, financials provide the indicators that leaders need to make informed decisions. Judge Jack Stack says, "Financials send messages about how to run a company. If your margins are low, you've got to do something about them. If you want to know the health of the company, look at the health of the balance sheet." Stack is an expert in using financials to guide business management. He pioneered the open-book management concept, which he calls his "mechanism for making sure reality smacks me in the face every single day." He explains: "Financials are like a crystal ball and they're telling you about the real things that are happening. Financial ratios tell you about how you need to guide and how you need to manage. If you do not listen to those financial ratios, you're not facing reality."

Stack adds that "statistics eliminate the emotion in leadership." Judge Victoria Jackson agrees and uses her own experience to illustrate: "In the early years, when a project was not performing as well as other projects, I had to back away and look at the numbers. If I saw that we weren't getting the best return on the capital we were investing, I would see if there was something we could do about it to change the situation. If we couldn't, I pulled the plug on it and moved on to the next thing." Jackson explained that cutting a project can be hard to do because it is easy to let ego get tied up into everything happening in your business.

MEET THE JUDGES

When it came to innovation and originality the first year I was judging, I really just looked at the concept. It hit me the second year to look at not just the uniqueness of the company but also the uniqueness of the individual. Now, I look to see how the entrepreneurs might have stepped outside the confines of their personal situation or accomplished what they did while dealing with what the organization presumed itself to be.

—**VICTORIA JACKSON**, President of Victoria Belle, Inc.

Victoria Jackson was invited to be an Entrepreneur Of The Year judge based on her expertise in the manufacturing industry. From 1977 until February 1999, Jackson was owner and chief executive officer at DSS/Pro Diesel, Inc., a diesel parts remanufacturing and distribution company. Today, she is president of Victoria Belle, Inc., a fine jewelry design and marketing firm.

Jackson took over DSS/Pro Diesel a few days before graduating from Belmont University. She astonished family and friends when she bought the outstanding shares of DSS and assumed her place as CEO shortly after the untimely death of her father, who founded the company.

Jackson serves as a past chair of the Committee of 200 and is a member of the board of directors of PepsiAmericas, Arvin Meritor, and AmSouth Bancorporation. She is the recipient of the 1990 Outstanding Business Leaders Award given annually by Northwood University and the 1990 Henry B. Sirotek Memorial Award, the highest honor bestowed by the Association of Diesel Specialists to a member whose efforts have produced significant advances either within the association or the industry.

In effect, understanding the financial performance of the various areas of their business allows successful entrepreneurs to bring a market mentality to their company. In their purest form, markets reward strong performance and punish laggards without emotion. The best managers use their knowledge of bottom-line results to incorporate a level of this efficiency into their own decision-making process. As a result, they are able to craft business strategies that more accurately reflect the reality of their marketplace—and are therefore more successful. But as Stack warns, "Once the financials tell you what to do, you have to have the guts to make the change."

Assuming that an entrepreneur has the courage to act on the basis of the financials, it's logical to conclude that his or her company will have an advantage over firms led by less financially astute individuals. Judge Ray Smilor confirms this, citing the results of a cooperative study between the Kauffman Center for Entrepreneurial Leadership and the Center for Creative Leadership. The study reports that accomplished entrepreneurs demonstrate three capabilities throughout each stage of their company's development. We covered the first two capabilities in Chapter 2: the ability to provide and articulate a vision and the ability to motivate and inspire others. The third capability is *financial know-how,* or the ability of entrepreneurs to understand the numbers of their own company and the critical factors that affect the bottom line.

A 2001 study by the Young Entrepreneurs Organization and the Kauffman Center for Entrepreneurial Leadership showed that the most successful entrepreneurs are those who are "deliberate and formal in strategic planning processes," a process that includes setting clear and measurable financial performance goals. By setting numerical targets, entrepreneurs provide a means of evaluating the performance of their company over the next year. Based on this performance, management can evaluate their strategy and see if any changes need to be made.

This kind of financial savvy is a distinguishing characteristic of Entrepreneur Of The Year winners.

Judge Jack Stack believes that your employees should also understand how financial indicators connect to their everyday activities. "You've got to teach people about financials. You have to engage them in the cash flow of the company," Stack says, speaking from experience.

In 1984 Stack acquired a failing company in which he had been a manager for years. He had earned the faith of about 250 employees who were counting on him to save their jobs. Stack quickly learned that he was "economically naïve." After years of managing money and people, he discovered that he didn't know anything about the business of business. He had put himself in charge of a company with almost $9 million of debt and didn't know anything about debt-to-equity ratios, liquidity ratios, balance sheets, or even business plans.

Of course, Stack was a quick study and the company he renamed SRC is now the holding company for 22 other businesses. Stack believes that if employees are financially literate, they are empowered every day to make decisions that strengthen the viability of a business. He adds: "I think financial performance is one of the single most important elements of leadership. If you are leading a group of people and taking them somewhere, your compass has got to be the financials. If you understand the numbers, then you will know what your overhead costs are, how much money you need to make every month, where that money comes from, what your margins are, and how to squeeze them if necessary."

PUTTING THE NUMBERS TO WORK

"The only way he might make it is if he's in a high-margin business and there's so much profit that when he makes a mistake, it covers itself up. Eventually, if he doesn't start running the company smart, the competition will catch on and eat it up."

—*JUDGE MILTON GRIEF*, when asked if a company can succeed if the entrepreneur doesn't have good financial management skills.

It's fine to say that business owners must let the financials guide their strategic decision making, but EOY judges are even more specific than that. They suggest specific methods and tools you can use in compiling and analyzing your numbers.

The daily demands of running a new business are more than enough to occupy an entrepreneur's full attention, often at the expense of financial management. As a company founder scrambles to make sure that contracts get signed and filled, he or she can get distracted from the critical task of monitoring the state and direction of the business as reflected by company financials. This mistake can be fatal, as revealed in the anecdote about judge Grief's friend, who concentrated on growing revenues without taking time to keep tabs on his accounts receivable.

But as all of the judges pointed out, monitoring your company's financial status is not necessarily a complex undertaking. It takes some degree of financial education and some sharp attentiveness. For example, one easy way to hear what the numbers are telling you is to incorporate milestones based on measures of financial performance into your business planning. These don't need to be intricate; often the simplest milestones are the most meaningful. For true start-ups, producing your first revenues is a clearly defined (and obviously important) goal. Once the revenues are flowing, you can shoot for a period of stable margins, your breakeven point, and ultimately sustainable profits.

But in order to make sense of even these basic goals, entrepreneurs must learn enough about basic finance to be able to understand a balance sheet, which lists all of a company's assets (including cash, inventory, facilities, equipment, patents owned, and accounts receivable), liabilities, and shareholders' equity. At the foundation of the balance sheet, which allows business owners to track and analyze general trends in their company, is a simple formula that reflects the general health or illness of the company: assets equal liabilities plus net worth (or shareholders' equity). If a company owes more in liabilities than the value of its assets, its net worth will be negative—a situation that cannot last indefinitely without outside financing.

In addition to the company's balance sheet, winning entrepreneurs also keep close tabs on their statements of income. These statements, commonly known as profit and loss statements, allow an entrepreneur to closely measure sales and expenses. The statement of income takes into account everything from net sales and margins to expenses and taxes in determining a company's net profit. By closely comparing income statements from one time period to the next, an entrepreneur can identify specific areas where expenses have increased. This will be critical information when drafting budgets and planning strategy for the future.

SMART FINANCIAL MANAGEMENT SYSTEMS

"Entrepreneurs always underestimate how long and how much it's going to take to get a job done."

—JUDGE ROBERT VUKOVICH

All of the EOY winners are familiar with financial statements and analyze them to gauge the current conditions of their business and guide their future strategies. But in light of the intense demands placed on entrepreneurs' time, they need a system to compile and consistently track their records accurately, so they can use them as an accurate, reliable, and constant guide.

Without exception, EOY winners have all created or appropriated simple and effective financial management systems. A good system measures a few key figures on a weekly, monthly, and quarterly basis. Any financial management system must be easy to use. The most financially efficient companies, whether small or large, have intuitive procedures and systems for reporting and accounting. For entrepreneurs, the judges say that this means picking one comprehensive accounting software package and sticking with it. It also means making sure that your financial measures are contained in a limited number of databases—ideally, just one. Whatever database application and other software you choose, the judges advise that you make sure it is compatible with Microsoft Excel, the most popular and easy-to-use spreadsheet application.

Using these tools, generating regular reports should not be too much of a drain on an entrepreneur's time. The clarity and comprehensiveness of a company's weekly, monthly, and quarterly financial reports can go a long way in impressing potential investors and, yes, even Entrepreneur Of The Year judges. These reports form key components of your communications with your existing investors, who want to keep close tabs on the progress of the company—or lack of it!

Weekly reports should include revenue and cost monitors that follow things like client cash in and personnel costs. Your monthly reports should measure your projected results versus your budgeted results. If you wait until the end of the year to see how performance matches up against past projections, it's too late. Quarterly reports should be more robust, with closing numbers on all key financial measures, analyses of margins (gross and operating), and an evaluation of the company's return on invested capital. This analysis should include an over-all measure of return on invested capital as well as breakdowns by product group or geographic area.

GROWTH IS GOOD . . . RIGHT?

"High-growth ventures have emerged as economic powerhouses in the United States, generating thousands of jobs, diffusing technological knowledge, and creating a culture of innovation that has ripple effects throughout every type of business organization. Indeed, their impact has changed business around the world."

—**DAVID BENDANIEL**, Professor of Entrepreneurship, Cornell University's Johnson Graduate School of Management (quoted by Nesheim)

The end goal of financial management is to turn your small business into a larger business, which requires *growth management,* the focus of this section. The quest for growth is universal, but it can also be dangerous. Unplanned growth can ruin a solid business just as quickly and as surely as a lack of sales. Growth without a foundation of good financial manage-ment can erode the health of even a dynamic young company, as evidenced by the case of judge Grief's financially distressed friend.

At many young companies, management sees growth as a panacea to any ills the firm might face. But in reality growth will not make up for a company's operational or financial shortcom-ings. In fact, it will exacerbate them. Growth will not necessarily even lead to more profits if a company spends too much to generate new business.

Throughout the 1990s, many businesses adopted a mind-set that growth in and of itself would determine which companies survived and which perished. By capturing enough market share, a company—especially an Internet company—could establish itself as the dominant force in the marketplace. Once that status was attained, everything else, from spiraling costs to elusive profits, would take care of itself—or so the theory went.

In the end it turned out that old-fashioned laws of business still rule. A company that's growing too quickly is prone to ignoring details and making mistakes. What's more, out-of-control growth makes life stressful for managers and employees, who begin to complain that their jobs aren't fun anymore. Every business should aim for *sustainable growth,* a term whose definition changes with each company. One company may find it difficult to sustain a growth rate of 10 percent, whereas another may be able to double or triple in size. Firms that successfully digest their growth tend to plan thoroughly and manage resources diligently.

When it comes to managing growth, Entrepreneur Of The Year judges sound two common themes:

1. Don't fall prey to overoptimistic assumptions.

2. Preserve capital.

Failed entrepreneurs tend to blame the demise of their business on a lack of sufficient capital. But the actual cause of disaster is more often a cash shortage caused at least in part by overly optimistic assumptions about costs, revenues, and profit margins; because this assessment of the cause of disaster is critical even when you are not focused on growth, we'll return to it.

However, when you are planning a growth strategy, EOY judges advise you to start with careful research about the financial realities of the industry you are entering. Are those 30 percent gross margins that you're predicting really feasible? By benchmarking your own growth rates, profit margins, and other measures of financial performance to those of your industry competitors, you can make certain that you're not viewing your own chance of success through rose-colored glasses.

Even if you do your research and put together what you think are reasonable growth projections, there's no guarantee that you will meet your goals. Sometimes there are unseen factors in your business that simply preclude growth beyond a certain point. Despite their success, all EOY winners have had to overcome the most common limiting factors to business growth: capital and management.

Acquiring the capital needed to fund your growth strategies is often the biggest problem. Borrowing money from banks to finance growth can be an easy option for a company with existing operations that produce an easily identifiable positive cash flow. If you're operating a chain of retail stores, for example, it's not hard to make a case that because each of your current locations generates a certain cash flow, you expect a new location to produce similar results. Problems arise when you're working with new business models, however. If your company is a content provider, it's much more difficult to pinpoint exactly how you'll generate a certain amount of cash flow through the injection of debt or even through an equity investment.

From a management perspective, the hardest aspect of growth is keeping your eye on the ball in the midst of expansion. In other words, when your business starts to grow, it's easy to get carried away. It's fun and exciting to spend your time acquiring new customers and scrambling to fill new orders. It's much less enjoyable, and considerably more challenging, to pay attention to the details that got your business off the ground in the first place.

In a small company, product quality and customer service are often the first casualties of rapid growth. Employee morale and corporate culture are generally the next to go, as your staff puts in long, stressful hours to keep up and new hires disrupt office stability. EOY judges unanimously cited the ability of entrepreneurs to grow their businesses while consistently maintaining or even improving the performance of current operations as a critical criterion in choosing the winners.

One way that EOY winners display their growth management ability is by guiding their companies past various inflection points in their growth cycles. When a business reaches an inflection point, it finds that it can no longer grow and expand with its current architecture. Sometimes this limitation arises from your systems or sometimes from your people. At this point, any business owner must make hard decisions to replace insufficient resources with more robust capacities. One common inflection point concerns information technology (IT) systems, which are often overwhelmed by an increase in data flow, an acquisition, or a shift in the business itself. If this occurs, smart entrepreneurs bring in experts to analyze whether it's possible to maintain or modify the existing system and still continue the desired level of growth. If the answer is no, smart entrepreneurs invest in new systems. The same decision-making process must hold for any business resource, including equipment, facilities, and even managers and employees.

BEA SYSTEMS, INC.

William T. Coleman III, founder, chairman, and chief strategy officer of BEA Systems, Inc., and the 2001 Entrepreneur Of The Year in technology and communications, understands how to make a company grow and how to manage that growth productively.

Coleman's skills in business strategy and operations, team building, and process management have been critical to his success. Since founding BEA in early 1995 with principals Ed Scott and Alfred Chuang, he has led the company to become the fastest software company to ever reach $1 billion in annual revenues, according to the firm's Web site. His leadership helped BEA—a world-leading e-business infrastructure software company and the market leader in Java applications—become one of the world's leading application infrastructure software companies.

Coleman, Scott, and Chuang founded the company in the belief that the Internet would need an operating system in the same way that personal computers do. They were right, and their vision has resulted in a company that some industry observers call the next Microsoft.

"It is all about an addressable opportunity, great people, focus, and execution," says Coleman of his success. "It's not magic." Perhaps not, but it *is* impressive. BEA has shown 22 straight quarters of record revenues.

According to its Web site, BEA has more than 12,500 customers, which it serves through 70 offices in 29 countries. BEA products and professional services let its customers integrate their packaged and legacy applications so they can automate business processes, share data, and find new uses for key information. BEA software also allows businesses to customize applications so they can open new sales channels, penetrate new markets, and even launch entirely new lines of business. In other words, BEA helps customers unleash the potential of the Internet.

Companies using BEA software can make rapid changes within their organization and achieve new levels of efficiency and responsiveness. BEA's application infrastructure simplifies the flow of information, decreases the costs of managing applications, and makes an enterprise more agile, productive, and connected. BEA's platform is the de facto standard for more than 2,100 systems integrators, independent software vendors, and application service providers.

But as with most Entrepreneur Of The Year winners, BEA and its CEO Alfred Chuang are also known for strong financial management and good corporate citizenship.

BEA's philanthropic efforts focus on early childhood learning because of its belief that healthy early development is the foundation for a person's lifelong success. In collaboration with both nonprofit and for-profit organizations, BEA takes a leadership role in developing and funding innovative programs that give young children a strong start in life and a solid foundation for their future success. Through grants made by the BEA Foundation, the company provides monetary support for programs that encourage positive and healthy learning among preschool children in the communities where BEA employees work and live. In addition to direct financial contributions, BEA donates software products to organizations that focus on early childhood learning or otherwise improve the quality of life for underserved populations.

To help individuals improve their community, the company assists employees with their own philanthropic efforts by providing paid time off for volunteer activities and by matching their charitable donations.

Bill Coleman carries out his own community service activities as president of the Colorado University Coleman Institute for Cognitive Disabilities Foundation and as a member of the board of directors of the Silicon Valley Manufacturing Group. Professionally, he focuses on strategic direction for BEA and works with the executive team to build relationships with customers and mentor employees, and promote the core values that inspire BEA's culture.

Prior to BEA, Coleman held various management positions at Sun Microsystems, Inc., and other high-technology companies, giving him more than 30 years of high-tech experience with particular emphasis on software development. A graduate of the U.S. Air Force Academy, he began his career in the U.S. Air Force as chief of satellite operations in the U.S. Office of the Secretary of the Air Force.

Coleman believes strongly that a solid company can only be built on a customer-focused culture that empowers people and rewards success. Therefore, BEA is working to build a business that can deliver leading products and services. According to the company's annual report, it has built a unique research and development organization through acquisition and hiring.

Though BEA's products often work behind the scenes, they are used by millions of people. The company intends its products to enable customers to maintain a competitive edge in the Internet era.

To reach more customers worldwide, BEA augmented its sales, services, and marketing teams by 66 percent to more than 750 professionals. It also formed strategic relationships with key partners in order to better leverage its direct sales capability. The results speak for themselves: Last year the company's revenues increased by more than 73 percent to more than $289 million, a true example of pace-setting growth and professional growth management.

SMART FINANCIAL PRACTICES

"Rule number one is never run out of cash. No matter how many grand ideas or visions you have, devote time to the issue of not running out of cash."

—JUDGE FEDERICO SANCHEZ

Now that we've uncovered some of the judges' thinking about growth and financial management, let's look at how Entrepreneur Of The Year winners actually display their financial acumen in starting their business and guiding its growth. In our discussions, the EOY judges identified a number of financial practices that they saw repeated in the management tactics of each of the EOY winners. In most cases, these common practices require only a basic financial education as opposed to an understanding of sophisticated financial techniques. These commonsense strategies described below are quite simple but are nevertheless often overlooked by entrepreneurs in their rush to make their business grow.

Pick a number.   Ray Smilor contends that the best way for entrepreneurs to incorporate financial elements into their overall management is to identify and track the two or three critical factors that really make the difference in performance. For some businesses, labor costs may be the critical factor. For others it may be inventory or the number of inbound sales calls. The important thing is that you are aware of the factors, know them, understand them, and communicate them to others in your organization. "Doing this can be very powerful," Smilor says. "Entrepreneurs who grasp how important the factors are can act very quickly and directly if the numbers indicate that a change is needed. They can allocate resources from one area to another to make sure critical factors get on track and stay there."

Preserve cash.   Many EOY judges echoed this bit of financial advice. "Cash is the hardest thing to get," according to judge Jim McCann. "Even if, for example, you have $100,000 and you need to get some equipment that costs $15,000, lease it and preserve the cash. It's almost impossible to have too much cash."

In 1997, Jonah Shacknai of Medics Pharmaceuticals Corporation was a national finalist in the EOY health care/life sciences category. Shacknai is a strong believer in retaining your cash by keeping overhead low, and his company does it by contracting for manufacturing, distribution, and research facilities instead of doing it all in-house. Outsourcing or contracting for services is a great way to get professional work without a large capital expenditure.

Most entrepreneurs view cash flow through the lens of burn rate. In other words, a new company is funded with a certain amount of capital, whether from the founder's life savings, family, friends, bank loans, or venture capitalists; and this capital must be spent to generate revenues. The amount of capital spent in excess of the amount of revenues produced in a given period is the company's *burn rate*. Initially, burn rate is generally high, as a fledgling business has little or nothing in the way of sales but faces substantial start-up costs. The burn rate should decline over time as sales build and costs level off, unless the company has decided on a fast-growth strategy, which will keep costs high. When revenues equal expenses, the company has reached breakeven.

No matter where a company sits on the breakeven continuum, maintaining ample cash to meet expenses is a paramount concern. In order to sufficiently gauge the amount of cash that a company will have on hand or tied up in its assets, entrepreneurs calculate liquidity measures. If you have outstanding corporate bank loans, you're probably familiar with the concept of *working capital,* which is simply a company's total of current assets less its current liabilities. Many loans stipulate that a company must maintain a certain minimum level of working capital.

Current ratio, which is determined by dividing a company's assets by its liabilities, tells a manager if a company has enough assets to safely cover foreseen debts and unforeseen costs. The results of this simple calculation are invaluable in making short-term strategic decisions about the direction of any business. For example, in most businesses, a current ratio of 2:1 is considered healthy. If a company's ratio were much lower than that, the company may want to consider paying down some debt or reinvesting some profits back into the business.

Entrepreneurs who obsess about their burn rates, liquidity ratios, and cash flows probably have the right mind-set, according to McCann, because "everything costs more than you think it will, and turning the corner takes longer than you think it will."

And as judge Stack warns, "When you're out of cash, you're out of air."

Let the numbers do the talking. Entrepreneur Of The Year judges are clear about the need to pay attention to your numbers and act on what they tell you without taking it personally. Judge Grief puts it this way: "Entrepreneurs sometimes operate from the heart, not the head. They want to grow or do this or that, but the numbers aren't there." Grief's advice is to let the numbers do the talking or risk "sabotaging your business in an effort to grow." If you want to add a million-dollar extension, he says, ask yourself: "Will your cash flows cover the costs? What kind of return would you get?"

As an example of how to make a smart business decision by the numbers, consider how Starbucks decides when to open a new store in a neighborhood that already has one. The company counts how many people are coming into the existing store and how long the customers have to wait. Once the wait gets too long, it's time to open another store nearby.

Even though that simple example focuses on some nonfinancial measures, managers can fall back on a plethora of financial methodologies that will help them determine the merit of various business options. All it takes is a consciousness about financial matters and a basic understanding of financial concepts. We've already discussed the importance of cash flow, which is critical to the survival of any business, from a hot dog vendor on the corner to a huge international corporation. Other basics that successful entrepreneurs watch closely are inventories, which often make up 50 percent of a company's assets, and accounts receivable, which, as noted earlier, can trip up even growing businesses.

Weigh your options. At a slightly more strategic level, EOY judges look for companies that use basic financial guideposts like net present value (NPV) and return on investment (ROI) in evaluating a company's options. The judges look for management teams that employ these two tools before putting capital into any new business or even a new venture within an existing company in order to asses the potential returns that such an investment will produce.

Net present value compares the value of a single dollar invested today with the value of that invested dollar at some point in the future, adjusted for the return and inflation. When making any investment decision, it's not enough to compare potential returns with the estimated cost of the capital you might invest. NPV allows you to make a more realistic analysis of the costs and potential benefits of any investment. If the NPV of a project is positive, the investment might be worthwhile. If the NPV is negative, the company's money can probably be better used elsewhere. Using this type of analysis allows you to compare the relative value of different investment options, such as hiring a new salesperson, buying a new piece of equipment, or embarking on a new marketing campaign.

When evaluating their investment in their company as a whole, entrepreneurs should look at ROI, which is calculated by dividing the company's pretax net profit by its net worth (equity). Once business owners or investors complete that calculation, they can then compare the result with other investment options. If the returns on less risky investments are greater than the return entrepreneurs are deriving from the business, entrepreneurs might seriously think about selling the company. This same type of analysis can be used to determine where capital should be allocated within the company itself.

Use your advisors. An entrepreneur's network is one of his or her most valuable assets. When it comes to making strategic decisions about financial management, an entrepreneur's key investors, board of directors, and board of advisors contribute experience, skill, and additional perspective.

In fact, setting up a knowledgeable and experienced team of advisors is a critical step in moving a business beyond the start-up stage. The expertise of your advisors can compensate for any of your own deficiencies in finance, strategy, and management or in knowledge of a particular industry or technology. In addition, the contacts that advisors provide serve as important sources of customers, employees, and—perhaps most important—funding.

The need for additional expertise often motivates entrepreneurs to bring in outside investors or venture capitalists. These professional investors sometimes have vast experience in running businesses or specific insight into a sector or market. In addition, they generally have access to proven executives who can be brought in to meet needs within your management team.

"A lot of times, people from lending institutions or other sources of capital offer assistance and advice if they think the entrepreneur is deficient in an area," says judge Victoria Jackson. Her advice: "Go along with those people. They're savvy, and they offer help because they believe in you and your idea."

THE JUDGES' BOTTOM LINE

"A giant company may be grossing billions of dollars, but when you really get down to the bottom line, its return might not be any higher than a stellar company doing $200 million. You see all this effort for such small return. Big revenues don't necessarily make a company great."

—JUDGE VICTORIA JACKSON

The story of judge Grief's friend whose business failed despite soaring sales demonstrates that superficial trappings of business success can mask deep-seated problems. So what are the signs that tell EOY judges whether a company is financially sound? When examining nominated companies, the judges focus on four main areas:

1. *Profit and gross profit margin.* Gross profit margin is expressed as a percentage, which is the gross profit divided by sales. Judge Carl Thoma says that any business that makes a 25 percent profit is doing something right. He adds that EOY judges ideally like to see a 30 percent before-tax profit and 20 percent after taxes. But in the end, the judges weigh a company based on the growth of its margins over a period and how its margins compare with those of its industry competitors. A 2001 study by the Young Entrepreneurs Organization and the Kauffman Center for Entrepreneurial Leadership showed that the average net profit margin for the lead-

ing entrepreneurial firms is five times greater than that of other new companies. Such higher profits mean that these companies don't have to borrow as frequently to fuel growth.

2. *Leverage.* You already know how EOY winners use debt and how EOY judges regard it, but remember that even if EOY judges don't mind leverage, they do keep a sharp eye out for excessive debt. Their main intent when looking at how debt factors into your company's capital structure is to be sure that your company is stable.

3. *Growth rate.* Growth rate is analyzed by examining earnings and revenue growth, with earnings growth usually the paramount consideration. In terms of top-line growth, EOY judges always carefully consider if revenue increases are the result of organic growth or if they are a result of acquisitions. "We need to determine if numbers like growth and revenue are due to activities such as expanding products and services to attract new customers or because of M&A activity," says judge Joanna Lau. Although acquisitions are by no means a negative factor, rapid internal growth is seen as a better indicator of corporate potential. In looking at the bottom line, the judges look for consistent growth as opposed to gains made through cost cutting.

   More than the mere existence of profit, judges want to see steady growth in earnings. They read repeated successes as a sign of viability and potential longevity. As judge William Mays explains: "We want to be sure that the company will be able to continue and thrive." Historical financial performance, such as year-to-year comparatives, is one of the most visible signs of whether a business is succeeding. Judge Sue Burnett says, "We saw a lot of candidates that, quite frankly, had good stories, but their company had been pretty flat for the last five to ten years."

4. *Return on Equity.* For publicly traded companies, the judges also assess return on equity, which is calculated by dividing a year's worth of earnings by the average shareholders' equity for that year. EOY judges prefer to see returns greater than 25 percent, especially in the younger companies.

In addition to these quantitative measures, the judges rely on their own experience and knowledge to assess the business fundamentals and financial management practices of the companies that they are asked to evaluate. For example, judge Jack Stack adds his own spin when determining the long-term viability of a business: "I look for the cash flow generators and the overhead absorbers. For example, is there a product, an idea, or a purchase order? Is the company going to be able to generate cash and absorb the overhead and expenses?"

When analyzing financial performance, "there is no absolute parameter," says judge Steve Papermaster. "Profit, however, is virtually a given. Our nominees have included candidates who haven't yet earned a profit, but, in general, most judges think that if a company isn't making money, it hasn't yet proved its business model."

But judge Victoria Jackson concludes that when trying to interpret the financial results of the EOY nominees, "what counts most is that the entrepreneur is being innovative and creative, and is able to keep reinventing the company when that's called for."

As almost all of the judges reminded us, numbers must be viewed in context so as not to be interpreted erroneously or reduced to meaningless information. Industry context is perhaps the most influential consideration. By inviting representatives from different industries to serve as EOY judges, we not only ensure that category winners are selected by a jury of their industry peers, but we also ensure that during the selection of the overall winner at least one judge is available as an industry specialist.

The industry specialist advises other judges about typical industry practices and benchmarks. As a result, judges are able to review candidate dossiers and identify unique or unusual developments or innovations that help to account for strong financial performance. In addition, the specialists are familiar with the standard business models in their industry, so they are able to relate a firm's financial performance and goals to its model and consider whether the performance is reasonable and sustainable.

Judge Victoria Jackson points out that the age of a company and where it is in its lifecycle also matter. She explains that judges don't expect a larger, older company to achieve the same growth rates as younger competitors. Judges are also aware that newer companies with double-digit revenue growth and profitability, although positioned to take off, are not out of the woods yet.

Ultimately, the EOY judges see financial performance as the final measure of a company's strategy and execution and thus the most important indicator of a company's merit and potential. Beyond the bottom line, the quality of financial management, to a great extent, determines an entrepreneur's ability to define his or her own corporate culture. "If a company has erratic earnings, it's hard to maintain a culture," says judge Carl Thoma. "It means you're hiring people one week and laying them off the next. It also means your strategy in the marketplace isn't giving you much control."

Clearly, this chapter isn't a practical guide to financial management. Rather, it provides some insight into the strategies, tools, and techniques that EOY winners used to attain success. In addition, hearing how EOY judges evaluate the financial practices of nominated companies helps explain how these factors contribute to a company's growth and survival and helps entrepreneurs identify the most critical elements of financial management for their own company.

In that spirit, note the words of judge Jack Stack: "If I give one piece of advice to entrepreneurs, it's to understand financial management. Take courses, go to school and open up the books inside your company. Don't give it to an accountant. Don't give it to a board of directors. Don't give it to the investment community. Study what it takes to financially engineer your company in line with your ideas."

CHAPTER SUMMARY

Most entrepreneurs don't possess the financial management skills required to achieve and sustain a competitive advantage. Entrepreneur Of The Year winners are an exception and have shown particular savvy at finding ways to achieve high growth, obtain capital without sacrificing voting control, and use equity and profit to selectively reward employees, advisors, and directors. To assess an EOY candidate's financial performance, judges look for steady growth in earnings. They also analyze a company's capital structure to make sure the company is stable and not overleveraged. For public companies, judges review return on equity. In assessing all of these measures, the judges take into consideration a company's industry and stage of development. Finally, the judges look for entrepreneurs who incorporate financial measures into their decision-making process so they can craft sound and successful strategies.

Job Interview Brainteasers

When William Saito looks for a new hire who is creative and innovative—someone to break the mold—he uses brain-teasing questions that he has collected. As he explains: "Some of the questions don't have a particular answer, but it's always interesting because you see not only the creativity of the person, but the personality. When a person keeps asking what about this, what about that, when he or she answers a question a certain way, it's all indicative of what a person's like, not only in terms of intellect, but personality." He divides his collection of brain teasers into general questions, applications, and thinkers.

GENERAL QUESTIONS

- Why is a manhole cover round?

- How many cars are there in the United States?

- You have two ropes (or fuses or whatever). Each requires one hour to burn completely. However, the ropes may burn irregularly such that half of a rope may burn in more or less than half an hour. You don't know the burning time of anything less than a full rope. How can you measure 45 minutes accurately with these ropes?

- You've got someone working for you for seven days and one gold bar to pay them. The gold bar is segmented into seven connected pieces. You must give them a piece of gold at the end of every day. If you are only allowed to make two breaks in the gold bar, how do you pay your worker?

- If you are on a boat and you throw out a suitcase, will the level of water increase?

- One train leaves Los Angeles at 15 mph heading for New York. Another train leaves from New York at 20 mph heading for Los Angeles on the same track. If a bird, flying at 25 mph, leaves from Los Angeles at the same time as the train and flies back and forth between the two trains until they collide, how far will the bird have traveled?

- You have ten tree seedlings to plant in your yard. How can you plant them in order to have five rows of four trees each?

- Three missionaries and three cannibals traveling together come to a river. They have only a small boat that will hold at most two people. Anybody can row the boat, but if cannibals ever outnumber missionaries on either side of the river, the cannibals will eat the missionaries. Otherwise, the cannibals are cooperative. How can they cross the river without anybody getting eaten?

- What is the product of $(x-a)(x-b)(x-c) \ldots (x-z)$?

- Take a 3-by-3 grid of evenly spaced points. On a piece of paper, draw four straight lines without lifting your pencil from the paper in such a way that they go through all nine points.

- Arrange the ten digits 0, 1, 2, 3, 4, 5, 6, 7, 8, 9 such that the first two of them form a number divisible by two, the first three form a number divisible by three, . . ., all ten digits form a number divisible by 10. (3816547290)

- You are applying for the position of the king's treasurer. As a test, the king has presented you with 12 gold coins and a balance (a scale that tells you only whether two things weigh the same or which one weighs more). One of the coins weighs slightly more or less than the others, but not by enough to determine it other than using the balance. Find the coin in three weighings and determine whether it is heavy or light. How can you arrange this to guarantee you can find the coin within three weighings?

- You succeed in doing so, but you are not the only applicant to do so, so the king presents you with a second test. This time, you have a new set of 13 coins, one of which is heavy or light, but not necessarily the same way as before, and the king also supplies you with one of the good coins from the first test, which weighs the same as the good coins in this test. How do you find the bad coin in three weighings and again determine whether it is heavy or light?

- You have two jars, 50 red marbles, and 50 blue marbles. A jar will be picked at random, and then a marble will be picked from the jar. Placing all of the marbles in the jars, how can you maximize the chances of a red marble being picked? What are the exact odds of getting a red marble using your scheme?

- Imagine you are standing in front of a mirror, facing it. Raise your left hand. Raise your right hand. Look at your reflection. When you raise your left hand your reflection raises what appears to be his right hand. But when you tilt your head up, your reflection does too and does not appear to tilt his or her head down. Why is it that the mirror appears to reverse left and right but not up and down?

- You have four jars of pills. Each pill is a certain weight, except for contaminated pills contained in one jar, where each pill is weight + 1. How can you tell which jar has the contaminated pills in just one measurement?

- If you had an infinite supply of water, and a five-quart and a three-quart pail, how would you measure exactly four quarts?

- You have a bucket of jellybeans. Some are red, some are blue, and some green. With your eyes closed, pick out two of a like color. How many do you have to grab to be sure you have two of the same color?

- Which way should the key turn in a car door to unlock it?

- If you could remove any of the 50 states, which state would it be and why?

- How many ping-pong balls will fit in this room?

- How many piano tuners are there in town?

- A room has three light bulbs. Outside are three switches, one for each bulb. You can't look at the lights when you flip a switch, only after you enter the room. Can you tell which switch controls which light with three looks? Two looks? One look?

- In Morse code a dot (•) can be sent in one time unit and a dash (–) can be sent in two time units. How many different messages can be sent in n time units?

- Given a rectangular (cuboidal for the puritans) cake with a rectangular piece removed (any size or orientation), how would you cut the remainder of the cake into two equal halves with one straight cut of a knife?

- How many points are there on the globe where by walking one mile south, one mile east, and one mile north you reach the place where you started?

- How would go about finding out where to find a book in a library? (You don't know how exactly the books are organized beforehand.)

APPLICATIONS

- Besides communication cost, what is the other source of inefficiency in RPC? How can you optimize the communication?

- How can computer technology be integrated in an elevator system for a hundred-story office building? How do you optimize for availability? How would variation of traffic over a typical workweek or floor or time of day affect this?

- A square picture is cut into 16 squares, and they are shuffled. Write a program to rearrange the 16 squares to get the original big square.

- How would you redesign an ATM?

- Suppose we wanted to run a microwave oven from the computer. What kind of software would you write to do this?

- How would you design a coffee machine for an automobile?

THINKERS

- How are M&Ms made?

- If you had to learn a new computer language, how would you go about doing it?

- If we told you we were willing to invest $5 million in a start-up of your choice, what business would you start? Why?

- If you could gather all of the computer manufacturers in the world together into one room and then tell them one thing that they would be compelled to do, what would it be?

- Explain a scenario for testing a saltshaker.

- If you are going to receive an award in five years, what is it for and who is the audience?

- How would you explain how to use Microsoft Excel to your grandmother?

- Why is it that when you turn on the hot water—in any hotel, for example—the hot water comes pouring out almost instantaneously?

- There are four people who need to cross a bridge at night. The bridge is only wide enough for two people to cross at once. There is only one flashlight for the entire group. When two people cross, they must cross at the slower member's speed. All four people must cross the bridge in 17 minutes, since the bridge will collapse in exactly that amount of time. Here are the times each member takes to cross the bridge:

Person A: 1 minute
Person B: 2 minutes
Person C: 5 minutes
Person D: 10 minutes

So, if persons A and C crossed the bridge initially, 10 minutes would elapse, because person C takes 10 minutes to cross. Then, person A would have to come back to the other side of the bridge, taking another minute, or 11 minutes total. Now, if persons A and D crossed the bridge next, it would take them 10 minutes, totaling 21 minutes, resulting in a collapsed bridge. How can all four people get across the bridge within 17 minutes? Note: You can't do tricky stuff like throwing the flashlight back from one end of the bridge to the other.

Interviews with Entrepreneur Of The Year judges

Books abstracted by GetAbstract.com:

Angel Investing: Matching Start-Up Funds with Start-up Companies: The Guide for Entrepreneurs, Individual Investors, and Venture Capitalists, Mark Van Osnabrugge and Robert J. Robinson (Jossey-Bass, 2000).

The Change Handbook: Group Methods for Shaping the Future, Peggy Holman and John Devane (Berrett-Koehler, 1999).

The Connected Corporation: How Leading Companies Win Through Customer-Supplier Alliances, Jordan D. Lewis (Free Press, 1995).

Finding and Keeping Great Employees, Jim Harris and Joan Brannick (Amacom, 1999).

The Future of Leadership: Today's Top Leadership Thinkers Speak to Tomorrow's Leaders, edited by Warren Bennis, Gretchen M. Sprietzer, and Thomas G. Cummings (Jossey-Bass, 2000).

The Guru Guide to Entrepreneurship: A Concise Guide to the Best Ideas from the World's Top Entrepreneurs, Joseph H. Boyett and Jimmie T. Boyett (John Wiley & Sons, 2000).

High Tech Start Up, John L. Nesheim (Free Press/Simon & Schuster, 2000).

Kotler on Marketing, Philip Kotler (Free Press, 1999).

Leadership: Enhancing the Lessons of Experience, Richard L. Hughes, Robert C. Ginnett, and Gordon J. Curphy (Irwin/McGraw-Hill, 1999).

Leading at the Edge: Leadership Lessons from the Extraordinary Saga of Shackleton's Antarctic Expedition, Dennis N.T. Perkins (Amacom, 2000).

Motivating Employees, Anne Bruce and James Pepitone (McGraw-Hill, 1999).

Nuts: Southwest Airlines' Crazy Recipe for Business and Personal Success, Kevin Frieberg and Jackie Frieberg (Bard Press, 1996).

The Passionate Organization: Igniting the Fire of Employee Commitment, James R. Lucas (Amacom, 1999).

The Real Work of Leaders: A Report from the Front Lines of Management, Donald L. Laurie (Perseus Books, 2000).

Rewarding Teams: Lessons from the Trenches, Glenn Parker, Jerry McAdams, and David Zielinski (Jossey-Bass, 2000).

The Stakeholder Strategy, Ann Svendson (Barrett-Koehler, 1998).

Twenty-Two Management Secrets to Achieve More with Less: Action Steps Leaders Take to Boost Productivity, John H. Zenger (McGraw-Hill, 1997).

GREGORY K. ERICKSEN, GLOBAL DIRECTOR, ENTREPRENEUR OF THE YEAR

Gregory K. Ericksen is the global director of Entrepreneur Of The Year (EOY) for Ernst & Young. During his 27-year career with Ernst & Young, Greg has also served as the firm's Indianapolis office managing partner, U.S. Midwest regional director of entrepreneurial services, and U.S. national director of entrepreneurial services.

In his role as global director of Entrepreneur Of The Year, Greg spearheads the international expansion of the Ernst & Young Entrepreneur Of The Year Awards. Greg has been a key player since the inception of the program in 1986 and has worked to expand Entrepreneur Of The Year to over 100 cities internationally in more than 30 countries around the world. Countries that host EOY or plan to initiate the event in the very near future include Australia, the Baltic states, Belgium, Brazil, Canada, the Caribbean, Chile, China, the Czech Republic, Denmark, Finland, France, Germany, Greece, India, Indonesia, Ireland, Italy, Japan, Malaysia, Mexico, the Netherlands, New Zealand, Norway, the Philippines, Portugal, Russia, Singapore,

South Africa, Spain, Sweden, Switzerland, Thailand, the United States, and the United Kingdom. Greg also serves as the chairman of the Entrepreneur Of The Year Academy, the governing body of the Entrepreneur Of The Year Hall of Fame—the exclusive organization of Entrepreneur Of The Year winners from around the world.

Three books profiling successful entrepreneurs have been authored by Greg, including *Net Entrepreneurs Only: 10 Entrepreneurs Tell the Stories of Their Success* (Wiley, 2000), *Women Entrepreneurs Only: 12 Women Entrepreneurs Tell the Stories of Their Success* (Wiley, 1999), and *What's Luck Got to Do With It?: 12 Entrepreneurs Reveal the Secrets Behind Their Success* (Wiley, 1997). He is also the coauthor of *The Ernst & Young Guide to Taking Your Company Public* (Wiley, 1995).

Greg is a Notre Dame graduate, where he received the Notre Dame Scholar Award, and has been a member of the Notre Dame Alumni Board of Directors.

Special Discounts

For special discounts
on 10 or more copies of
*The Ernst & Young
Entrepreneur Of The Year® Award
Insights from the Winner's Circle,*
please call Dearborn Trade
Special Sales at
800-621-9621, ext. 4307.

Dearborn™
Trade Publishing
A **Kaplan Professional** Company